Math 2
An Incremental Development

Student Workbook (Part One)

Nancy Larson

with

Roseann Paolino

Saxon Publishers, Inc.

Math 2: An Incremental Development

Student Workbook

Printed in the United States of America

ISBN: 0-939798-82-4

Editor: Deborah Williams
Production Supervisor: David Pond
Graphic Artists: Scott Kirby, John Chitwood, Gary Skidmore,
                 Tim Maltz, and Chad Threet

Manufacturing Code: 07S0500

┌─ *Reaching us via the Internet* ─┐
│   │
│ **WWW:** http://www.saxonpub.com │
│ **E-mail:** info@saxonpub.com   │
└───────────────────────────────────┘

Saxon Publishers, Inc.
2450 John Saxon Blvd.
Norman, OK 73071

TO THE TEACHER

Each of Saxon Publishers' two-part student workbooks contains all the necessary material for one student for the entire year. In addition to the actual student material, we have included several items that we hope will be of use to you.

The pages immediately following are an assortment of recording forms developed for your convenience. The workbooks are designed for use in classrooms of all sizes. In addition, throughout each workbook, written assessments appear in the sequentially correct locations.

In order to better maintain control of the student materials, we suggest that you not distribute the workbooks to your students. As you know, young children often misplace school materials. Also, if given access to an entire semester's materials, some students will attempt to work ahead of the class. By removing each day's necessary pages from each workbook and distributing them to the students yourself, these possibilities are eliminated.

Of course, every classroom is different. If you find it necessary or desirable to distribute the workbooks to the students, remove the recording forms first. Please keep in mind that the written assessments are contained in the workbooks.

MATH 2
HOMEWORK RECORDING FORM

Teacher _____

Date _____

Students	Practice Sheet #																		

2-PFg

MATH 2
ASSESSMENT RECORDING FORM
Semester 1   (Lessons 1 - 70)

Teacher _____

Date _____

Students	\multicolumn{13}{c}{Assessment}
	1	2	3	4	5	6	7	8	9	10	11	12	13

MATH 2
ASSESSMENT RECORDING FORM
Semester 2   (Lessons 71 - 132)

Teacher _____

Date _____

Students	Assessment											
	14	15	16	17	18	19	20	21	22	23	24	25

2-PFi

Math 2

Class Fact Sheet Recording Form (page 1)
Semester 1 (Lessons 1 - 70)

Date _____

Teacher _____

Students	AA 1.0	A 1.2	A 2.0	A 2.2	A 3.0	A 3.2	AA 4.0	A 4.0	A 4.2	A 5.1	A 5.2

2-PFj

Math 2

Class Fact Sheet Recording Form (part) Semester 1 (Lessons 1 - 70)

Teacher _____

Date _____

Students	MA 6.0	A 6.2	A 7.1	A 7.2	A 8.1	A 8.2	S 1.2	S 2.0	S 3.2	S 3.4	S 4.0

Math 2

Class Fact Sheet Recording Form (page 1)   Teacher _____   Date _____
Semester 2   (Lessons 71 - 132)

Students	S 4.0	S 4.4	S 5.0	S 5.4	S 6.0	S 6.4	S 7.0	S 7.4	S 8.0	S 8.1

Class Fact Sheet Recording Form (page 2)
Semester 2   (Lessons 71 - 132)

Teacher _____

Date _____

Students	S 8.2	M 10.0	M 11.0	M 13.0	M 14.0	M 14.1	M 15.0	M 17.0	A1-100	A2-100	S-100

Child's Name _____

LESSON 10 – Oral Assessment #1   Date _____

Counting by 10's; Identifying and Writing Numbers to 100

Materials:
hundred number chart
handwriting paper
pencil

	•Use the hundred number chart. *"Point to the number…"* *"…17."* *"…82."* *"…to the right of 65."* *"…to the left of 23."*	*"Write these numbers."* *"32, 71, 80, 16, 53, 12, 19."*
"Count by 10's to 100."		

LESSON 20 – Oral Assessment #2   Date _____

Identifying Days of the Week; Identifying Ordinal Position

Materials:
pattern blocks

A. *"Name the days of the week."* B. *"What are the weekdays?"* C. *"What are the days of the weekend?"*			•Place 12 pattern blocks in a row. *"Point to the first block."* *"Point to the fourth, …eighth, …eleventh."*
A.	B.	C.	

LESSON 30 – Oral Assessment #3   Date _____

Identifying Attributes of Shapes; Making up Addition and Subtraction Stories

Materials:
shape pieces from Lesson 22

•Use the shape pieces from Lesson 22. •Choose two pieces that differ by color and size. A. *"How are these pieces the same?"* B. *"How are they different?"*		A. *"Make up a some, some more story."* B. *"Make up a some, some went away story."*	
A	B	A	B

LESSON 40 – Oral Assessment #4   Date _____

Counting Backward by 10's; Counting by 5's; Showing Money Amounts Using Dimes and Pennies

Materials:
10 dimes
10 pennies

A. *"Count backward from 100 by 10's."* B. *"Count by 5's to 50."*		A. *"Show 13¢."* B. *"Show 40¢."* C. *"Show 67¢."*		
A	B	A	B	C

Child's Name _____

● **LESSON 50 – Oral Assessment #5**   Date _____

Identifying the Months of the Year;
Identifying Halves, Fourths, and Eighths.

Materials:
individual fraction
piece set (from
Lesson 34)

A. *"Name the months of the year."* B. *"What is the ___th month of the year?"*	*"Which piece is one half of the yellow?"* *"Which piece is one fourth of the yellow?"* *"Which piece is one eighth of the yellow?"* *"Cover the yellow circle using eighths."* *"How many eighths did you use?"* •Repeat with fourths.

A	B

LESSON 60 – Oral Assessment #6   Date _____

Counting by 1's; Showing Time to the Half Hour

Materials:
individual clocks

A. *"Count by 1's from 90 to 120."* B. *"Count by 1's from 590 to 620."*		A. *"Show half past seven on the clock."* B. *"Show the time one hour ago."*	
A	B	A	B

•Reassess the child on questions answered incorrectly (or not answered) on
Assessments 1–5.

LESSON 70 – Oral Assessment #7   Date _____

Making Congruent Shapes; Dividing a Shape in Half

Materials:
Teacher Master 2-70
geoboard
5 geobands

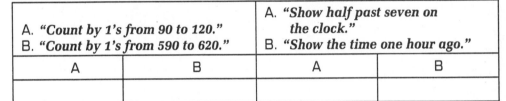

• Show the child a copy of Teacher's Master 2-70. • Give the child a geoboard and geobands. *"Copy this shape on your geoboard."*	• Make the following rectangle on a geoboard. • Give the child another geoboard. *"Use this band to divide the rectangle in half."* *"Can you divide it in half a different way?"*

Child's Name _____

LESSON 80 – Oral Assessment #8   Date _____

Making and Reading a Graph

Materials:
baskets of
color tiles of
mixed colors

"Take a double handful of color tiles."
A. *"Make a graph to show the colors of the tiles you picked."*
• Allow time for the child to make the graph.
B. *"Tell me about your graph."*
C. *"How many more _____ tiles are there than _____ tiles?"*

A. Graphs with 1–1 Correspondence	**B.** Describes the Graph	**C.** Compares Columns

LESSON 90 – Oral Assessment #9   Date _____

Identifying Even and Odd Numbers;
Reading a Thermometer to the Nearest 2°

Materials:
thermometer

"What are the even numbers?" • Stop child's counting at 20. *"What are the odd numbers?"* • Stop child's counting at 19.	• Show the child the thermometer. *"What is the temperature?"* • Accept answers to the nearest 2°.

LESSON 100 – Oral Assessment #10   Date _____

Modeling and Describing Addition with Regrouping

Materials:
10 dimes
20 pennies
scrap paper

"Show me 36¢." • Hand the child 47¢. *"How much money did I give you?"* *"Show that using the fewest number of pennies."*		• Write 36¢ + 47¢ on a piece of scrap paper. *"Show how to find the answer for this example."* *"Explain each step."*		
Counts Money	Trades Pennies for Dimes	Sets Up Example	Adds Correctly	Explains Steps (References Money)

Child's Name _____

LESSON 110 – Oral Assessment #11   Date _____

Reading and Showing Time to 5-Minute Intervals

Materials: demonstration clock individual clock	• Show a time to a five-minute interval on the demonstration clock. *"It's morning."* *"What time is it?"*	• Give the child an individual clock. *"Show five forty-five on your clock."* (Vary the time used.)

LESSON 120 – Oral Assessment #12   Date _____

Modeling and Describing Subtraction with Renaming

Materials: 10 dimes 20 pennies scrap paper	*"Put 52¢ on the paper."* *"Give me 15¢ of that money."* *"How much money do you have left?"*			• Write 52¢ – 15¢ on a piece of scrap paper. *"Show how to find the answer for this example."* *"Explain each step."*		
	Recognizes that Trading is Necessary	Trades a Dime for 10 Pennies	Gives Away 15¢	Counts Money	Trades Correctly	Subtracts Correctly	Explains Steps

LESSON 130 – Oral Assessment #13   Date _____

Counting and Showing Money Amounts to $1.00

Materials: 5 quarters 10 dimes 10 nickels 20 pennies	• Hand the child a selection of coins including at least one of each coin with a total value less than $1.00. *"Count the money."*	*"Show 82¢."* (Vary the amounts for different children.) *"Show 82¢ using different coins."*

• Reassess the child on questions answered incorrectly (or not answered) on Assessments 1–12.

Math 2

Individual Recording Form
Semester 1 (Lessons 1-70)

School Year _____ Name _____

Teacher _____

Written Assessments — Comments/Missed Items

#	Comments/Missed Items
1	
2	
3	
4	
5	
6	
7	
8	
9	
10	
11	
12	
13	

Fact Sheets — 1-minute timings

Addition (# correct/25)

AA 1.0	A 5.1					
A 1.2	A 5.2					
A 2.0	MA 6.0					
A 2.2	A 6.2					
A 3.0	A 7.1					
A 3.2	A 7.2					
AA 4.0	A 8.1					
A 4.0	A 8.2					
A 4.2						

Subtraction (# correct/25)

S 1.2						
S 2.0						
S 3.2						
S 3.4						
S 4.0						

Record the number of facts answered correctly in 1 minute.

Target number of facts answered correctly in 1 minute.

20-25 excellent
15-19 good
10-14 acceptable

Oral Assessments   Notes and Comments

1	
2	
3	
4	
5	
6	
7	

Math 2   *Individual Recording Form*
Semester 2 (Lessons 71-132)

School Year _____   Name _____

Teacher _____

Fact Sheets — 1-minute timings

Subtraction (# correct/25)					Multiplication (# correct/25)				
S 4.0					M 10.0				
S 4.4					M 11.0				
S 5.0					M 13.0				
S 5.4					M 14.0				
S 6.0					M 14.1				
S 6.4					M 15.0				
S 7.0					M 17.0				
S 7.4					5-minute timings				
S 8.0					A1-100				
S 8.1					A2-100				
S 8.2					S-100				

Record the number of facts answered correctly in 1 minute.

Target number of facts answered correctly in 1 minute.

20-25 excellent
15-19 good
10-14 acceptable

Record the number of facts answered correctly in 5 minutes.

90-100 excellent
80-89 good
70-79 acceptable

Written Assessments — Comments/Missed Items

14	
15	
16	
17	
18	
19	
20	
21	
22	
23	
24	
25	

2-PFt

Oral Assessments

Notes and Comments

8	
9	
10	
11	
12	
13	

Dear Parent,

Each day your child will participate in a wide variety of mathematics activities. Your child will learn through hands-on experiences, discussion, and exploration. The new learning will be reinforced through carefully considered practice.

Our day begins with The Meeting. This is a time when we practice a wide variety of every day skills. A "Student of the Day" assists in asking questions about the calendar, time, temperature, pattern of the day, classroom graphs, and money.

The next part of *Math 2* is the Lesson. During the Lesson a new concept is presented through discussion and an activity. Concepts and skills in *Math 2* include computation, problem solving strategies, measurement, geometry, money, time, identifying patterns, fractions, graphs, and charts.

Number facts are introduced using fact strategies and are practiced throughout the year. The children compete only against themselves and strive to improve their own scores on fact sheets. Children are encouraged to practice the number facts at home through games and activities.

After each lesson we will practice the new learning, as well as concepts previously introduced, through guided written practice. The children complete and correct Side A of a practice sheet in class. Side B is your child's homework. The examples are similar to those on side A.

Your child will have homework 3–4 nights a week. Please assist your child by reading the problems on Side B, if necessary. Allow your child to arrive at the answers independently. Check your child's work and help your child correct mistakes. If you helped your child with an example, please circle the problem number to let me know that this is a difficult question. It is important that your child return the homework the next day.

Assessment of your child's progress occurs every five lessons. Each written assessment includes skills your child has been practicing throughout the year. We will strive for 80 percent mastery on all assessments. Any missed objectives will be reviewed and retaught. During our conferences, I will share with you my observations about your child's progress.

Please contact me if you have any questions about the program or your child's progress.

Sincerely,

Name _____

Date _____

1. What day of the week is it today? _____

2. Write the letter **e** to the right of the **n**.

    Write the letter **o** to the left of the **n**.

    ____   n   ____

3. Use a red crayon to color these numbers on the chart.
    Cross off each number after you color it.

    14, 1, 28, 10, 17, 5, 34, 12, 23
    50, 19, 46, 37, 6, 45, 32, 39, 41

1	2	3	4	5	6	7	8	9	10
11	12	13	14	15	16	17	18	19	20
21	22	23	24	25	26	27	28	29	30
31	32	33	34	35	36	37	38	39	40
41	42	43	44	45	46	47	48	49	50

4. What number is one more than **28**? _____

    What number is one less than **37**? _____

2-2Wa

1. Read these numbers to someone.

$$39, 18, 12, 22, 40, 48$$

2. Write the letter **t** to the left of the **w**.

   Write the letter **o** to the right of the **w**.

   _____   W   _____

3. Use a red crayon to color these numbers on the chart.
   Cross off each number after you color it.

   22, 14, 37, 8, 23, 34, 42, 17, 48, 6
   12, 44, 27, 46, 4, 32, 47, 7, 24, 2

1	2	3	4	5	6	7	8	9	10
11	12	13	14	15	16	17	18	19	20
21	22	23	24	25	26	27	28	29	30
31	32	33	34	35	36	37	38	39	40
41	42	43	44	45	46	47	48	49	50

Name _____

● Date _____

1. Use the class birthday graph to answer these questions.

    How many children have birthdays in October? _____

    What months do not have birthdays?

    _____

2. What number is one less than **13**? _____

    What number is one more than **20**? _____

● 3. Count from one to twenty. Write the numbers.

    _____ , _____ , _____ , _____ , _____ , _____ , _____ , _____ , _____ , _____

    _____ , _____ , _____ , _____ , _____ , _____ , _____ , _____ , _____ , _____

4. Write the digital time.

    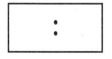

5. Write the letter **s** to the left of the **c**.
    Write the letter **h** to the right of the **c**.
    Write the letter **o** to the left of the **l**.

●

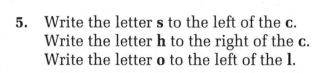
____ c ____ o ____ l

Name _____ **LESSON 3B**
                                                Math 2
Date _____

1. What will be tomorrow's date?

   _____

2. What number is one less than **25**? _____

   What number is one more than **16**? _____

3. Count backward from twenty to one. Write the numbers.

   __20__ , _____ , _____ , _____ , _____ , _____ , _____ , _____ , _____ , _____

   _____ , _____ , _____ , _____ , _____ , _____ , _____ , _____ , _____ , _____

4. Write the digital time.

   [:]

5. Write the letter **u** to the left of the **s**.
   Write the letter **e** to the right of the **s**.
   Write the letter **h** to the left of the **o**.

   ____ ____ O ____ S ____

Name _____   **LESSON 4A**
                                                   Math 2
● Date _____

1. What day of the week is it today? _____

    What day of the week was it yesterday? _____

2. Write the letter **h** to the left of the **o**.

    Write the letter **t** to the right of the **o**.   ___ $\underset{o}{\_\_\_}$ ___

3. Fill in the missing numbers.

    _1_ , _2_ , ___ , _4_ , ___ , ___ , _7_ , ___ , _9_ , ___

    ___ , ___ , _13_ , ___ , ___ , ___ , ___ , _18_ , ___ , ___

● 4. What number is one less than **26**? _____

    What number is one more than **43**? _____

5. Use an orange crayon to color these numbers on the chart.

    23, 42, 37, 8, 29, 4, 2   16 + 1   26 + 1   9 + 1   4 + 1

    41, 43, 45, 3, 28, 9, 1   32 + 1   46 + 1   43 + 1   12 + 1   6 + 1

1	2	3	4	5	6	7	8	9	10
11	12	13	14	15	16	17	18	19	20
21	22	23	24	25	26	27	28	29	30
31	32	33	34	35	36	37	38	39	40
41	42	43	44	45	46	47	48	49	50

2-4Wa

Name _____

Date _____

1. What will be tomorrow's date? _____

2. Write the letter **t** to the left of the **o**.

   Write the letter **e** to the right of the **o**.

   ____ o ____

3. Fill in the missing numbers.

   _1_ , ___ , _3_ , ___ , ___ , ___ , ___ , _8_ , ___ , ___

   ___ , _12_ , ___ , ___ , ___ , _16_ , ___ , ___ , ___ , ___

4. What number is one more than **76**? _____

   What number is one less than **52**? _____

5. Fill in the missing numbers.

1	2		4	5		7		9	10
		13		15			18		
21		23			26			29	
	32			35				39	
41			44		46	47			50

Name _____

Date _____

1. Fill in the missing days of the week.

   Sunday, _____, Tuesday, _____,

   Thursday, _____, Saturday

2. Which letter is on the right? _____   e i p

   Which letter is in the middle? _____

   Which letter is on the left? _____

3. Use the birthday graph to answer these questions.

   How many birthdays are in June? _____

   Which month has the most birthdays? _____

4. Count by 10's. Write the numbers.

   _10_ , _20_ , _____, _____, _____, _____, _____, _____, _____, _____

5. Fill in the missing numbers.

1	2	3	4	5	6	7	8	9	10
21	22	23	24	25	26	27	28	29	30
41	42	43	44	45	46	47	48	49	50

1. Fill in the missing days of the week.

    _____, Monday, _____, Wednesday

    _____, Friday, _____

2. Which letter is on the left? _____   b   y   o

    Which letter is on the right? _____

    Which letter is in the middle? _____

3. Fill in the missing numbers.

    __1__ , __2__ , _____ , _____ , _____ , _____ , _____ , __8__ , __9__ , _____

    _____ , _____ , __13__ , _____ , _____ , __16__ , _____ , _____ , __19__ , _____

4. Count backward by 10's. Write the numbers.

    __100__ , __90__ , __80__ , _____ , _____ , _____ , _____ , _____ , _____ , _____

5. Fill in the missing numbers.

1	2	3	4		6	7	8	9	
11	12	13	14		16	17	18	19	
21	22	23	24		26	27	28	29	
31	32	33	34		36	37	38	39	
41	42	43	44		46	47	48	49	

3	5	2	1	4
+ 3	+ 5	+ 2	+ 1	+ 4

0	4	5	3	1
+ 0	+ 4	+ 5	+ 3	+ 1

2	5	3	0	1
+ 2	+ 5	+ 3	+ 0	+ 1

4	3	5	2	0
+ 4	+ 3	+ 5	+ 2	+ 0

1	4	2	3	5
+ 1	+ 4	+ 2	+ 3	+ 5

Score: _____

2-6Fa

Name _____

● Date _____

1. Fill in the missing days of the week.

   Tuesday, _____, _____, Friday

2. Draw a square to the left of the circle.
   Draw a triangle to the right of the circle.

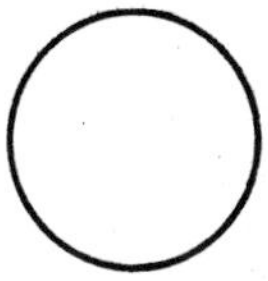

3. Use the birthday graph to answer these questions.

   How many birthdays are in February? _____

   Which months have exactly two birthdays?

● _____

4. Count backward by 10's. Write the numbers.

   100 , 90 , 80 , ____, ____, ____, ____, ____, ____, ____

5. Show | 2:00 |

2-6Wa

1. Fill in the missing days of the week.

   _____, Wednesday, Thursday, _____

2. Draw a circle to the right of the square.
   Draw a triangle to the left of the square.

3. Fill in the missing numbers.

   ____, ____, ____, ____, 5 , ____, ____, 8 , ____, ____

   11 , ____, 13 , ____, ____, ____, ____, 18 , ____, ____

4. Count by 10's. Write the numbers.

   10 , 20 , 30 , ____, ____, ____, ____, ____, ____, ____

5. Show | 8:00 |

6	3	9	1	7
+ 6	+ 3	+ 9	+ 1	+ 7

4	8	6	9	0
+ 4	+ 8	+ 6	+ 9	+ 0

2	7	5	3	4
+ 2	+ 7	+ 5	+ 3	+ 4

8	6	1	9	5
+ 8	+ 6	+ 1	+ 9	+ 5

0	2	7	4	8
+ 0	+ 2	+ 7	+ 4	+ 8

Score: _____

Name _____ **LESSON 7A**

Date _____ *Math 2*

1. Fill in the missing days of the week.

   _____, Monday, _____, _____

   Thursday, _____, _____

2. Write an **i** on the second line.
   Write a **t** on the fifth line.
   Write a **g** on the third line.   _____ _____ _____ _____ _____
   Write an **h** on the fourth line.
   Write an **r** on the first line.

3. Write the numbers that are one less.

   _____, 28   _____, 16

4. Write the digital time.

   ┌─────────┐
   │   :   │
   └─────────┘

5. Find the answers.

$$\begin{array}{cccccccc} 4 & \quad 7 & \quad 3 & \quad 9 & \quad 6 & \quad 2 & \quad 8 \\ +\,4 & +\,7 & +\,3 & +\,9 & +\,6 & +\,2 & +\,8 \\ \hline \end{array}$$

1. Fill in the missing days of the week.

   Sunday, _____, _____, _____

   _____, Friday, _____

2. Write an **e** on the third line.
   Write an **a** on the fourth line.
   Write a **g** on the first line.   _____ _____ _____ _____ _____
   Write a **t** on the fifth line.
   Write an **r** on the second line.

3. Write the numbers that are one less.

   _____, 39   _____, 12

4. Write the digital time.

   [__ : __]

5. Find the answers.

5	1	8	3	6	10	7
+ 5	+ 1	+ 8	+ 3	+ 6	+ 10	+ 7

6 + 6	3 + 3	9 + 9	1 + 1	7 + 7
4 + 4	8 + 8	6 + 6	9 + 9	0 + 0
2 + 2	7 + 7	5 + 5	3 + 3	4 + 4
8 + 8	6 + 6	1 + 1	9 + 9	5 + 5
0 + 0	2 + 2	7 + 7	4 + 4	8 + 8

Score: _____

1. Use the birthday graph to answer these questions.

    What is the first month of the year? _____

    How many children have a birthday in that month? _____

2. One of these is my dog.
    Use the clues to find my dog.
    He is not second. Cross out that dog.
    He is not on the left. Cross out that dog.
    Circle my dog.

3. Circle the greater number.

    24   17

4. Show | 5:00 | on the clock.

5. Continue the repeating pattern.

    ⟨○⟩ , ⟨□⟩ , ⟨○⟩ , ⟨□⟩ , _____ , _____ , _____ , _____ , _____ , _____

6. Fill in the missing numbers.

1		3		5		7		9	
11		13		15		17		19	
21		23		25		27		29	

2-8Wa

Name _____

Date _____

1. What will be tomorrow's date? _____

2. One of these is my grandmother's dog.
    Use the clues to find her dog.
    She is not third. Cross out that dog.
    She is not on the left. Cross out that dog.
    Circle her dog.

3. Circle the greater number.

    38   43

4. Show | 4:00 | on the clock.

5. Continue the repeating pattern.

    △ , ○ , △ , ○ , ____ , ____ , ____ , ____ , ____ , ____

6. Fill in the missing numbers.

	2		4		6		8		10
12		14		16		18		20	
22		24		26		28		30	

4 + 1	8 + 1	1 + 2	5 + 1	1 + 7
9 + 1	1 + 1	1 + 6	3 + 1	1 + 9
1 + 3	4 + 1	1 + 0	6 + 1	5 + 1
1 + 5	8 + 1	2 + 1	1 + 7	1 + 1
9 + 1	1 + 6	5 + 1	1 + 0	1 + 1

Score: _____

Name _____

Date _____

1. Use the birthday graph to answer the questions.

   How many children have birthdays in August? _____

   What is the fourth month of the year? _____

   How many children have birthdays in that month? _____

2. Count by 10's. Fill in the missing numbers.

   10, _____, _____, _____, _____, _____, _____, _____, _____, _____

3. Show $\boxed{9\!:\!00}$ on the clock.

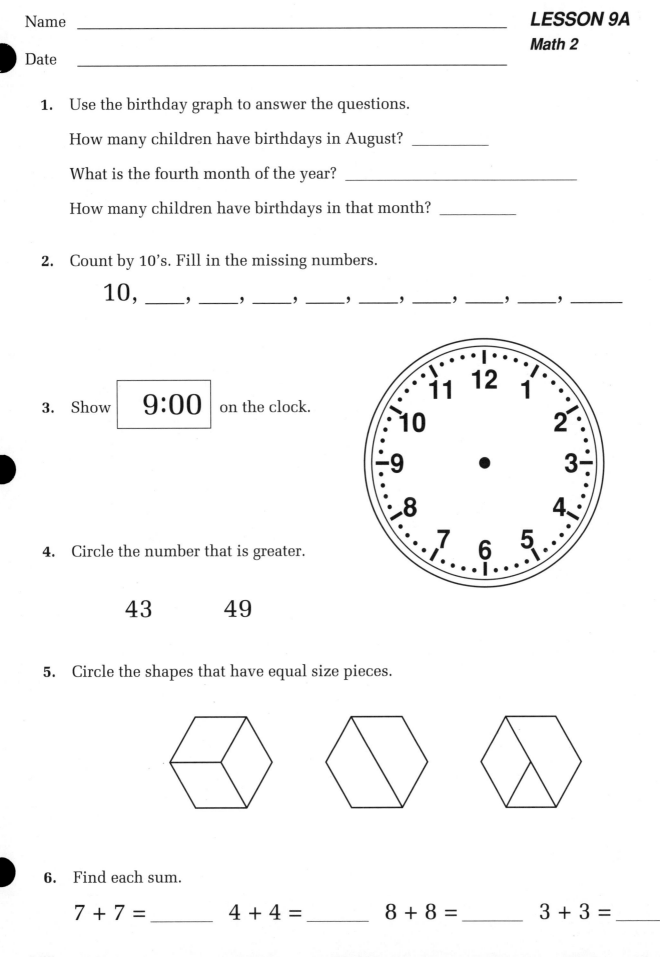

4. Circle the number that is greater.

   43   49

5. Circle the shapes that have equal size pieces.

6. Find each sum.

   7 + 7 = _____   4 + 4 = _____   8 + 8 = _____   3 + 3 = _____

Name _____

Date _____

1. What will be tomorrow's date? _____

2. Count backward by 10's. Fill in the missing numbers.

    100, ____, ____, ____, ____, ____, ____, ____, ____, ____

3. Show [1:00] on the clock.

4. Circle the number that is greater.

    58   54

5. Circle the shapes that have equal size pieces.

6. Find each sum.

    $5 + 5 =$ _____ $9 + 9 =$ _____ $2 + 2 =$ _____ $6 + 6 =$ _____

Name _____

● Date _____

1. Use the birthday graph to answer the questions.

   How many children have birthdays in September? _____

   What month has the most birthdays? _____

2. Finish the repeating pattern.

   □ , ○ , □ , ○ , _____ , _____ , _____ , _____ , _____ , _____

3. What number is one more than **34**? _____

   What number is one less than **54**? _____

4. Show | 10:00 | on the clock.

5. Fill in the missing numbers.

1	2			5			8		
		13				17			20
21			24		26				

6. Find each sum.

   2 + 2 = _____   5 + 5 = _____   8 + 8 = _____   3 + 3 = _____

   7 + 7 = _____   4 + 4 = _____   9 + 9 = _____   6 + 6 = _____

Name _____

How many blocks of each
color did you use?

yellow _____

red _____

blue _____

green _____

orange _____

tan _____

How many blocks of each
color did you use?

yellow _____

red _____

blue _____

green _____

orange _____

tan _____

Name _____

A 1.2

```
   6        3        9        1        7
 + 6      + 3      + 9      + 1      + 7
 ____     ____     ____     ____     ____

   4        8        6        9        0
 + 4      + 8      + 6      + 9      + 0
 ____     ____     ____     ____     ____

   2        7        5        3        4
 + 2      + 7      + 5      + 3      + 4
 ____     ____     ____     ____     ____

   8        6        1        9        5
 + 8      + 6      + 1      + 9      + 5
 ____     ____     ____     ____     ____

   0        2        7        4        8
 + 0      + 2      + 7      + 4      + 8
 ____     ____     ____     ____     ____
```

Score: _____

2-10Fa

6 + 6	3 + 3	9 + 9	1 + 1	7 + 7
4 + 4	8 + 8	6 + 6	9 + 9	0 + 0
2 + 2	7 + 7	5 + 5	3 + 3	4 + 4
8 + 8	6 + 6	1 + 1	9 + 9	5 + 5
0 + 0	2 + 2	7 + 7	4 + 4	8 + 8

Score: _____

1. One of these is my favorite color. Use the clues to find my favorite color.

   | red | | blue | | yellow | | green |

   It is not third. Cross out that color.

   It is not on the right. Cross out that color.

   It is not first. Cross out that color.

   Circle my favorite color.

2. Circle the smaller number.

   28   34

3. Finish the repeating pattern.

   △, ○, ○, △, ○, ○, __, __, __, __, __, __

4. What number is one more than **63**? _____

   What number is one less than **47**? _____

5. Find the number that belongs in the square with the **A**. _____

   Find the number that belongs in the square with the **B**. _____

   Fill in the missing numbers.

1	2			5					10
		13							
				A	26				
31			34						40
41					B			49	50

Name _____ **LESSON 11B**

Date _____ **Math 2**

1. One of these is my sister's favorite color. Use the clues to find my sister's favorite color.

    | red | | blue | | yellow | | green |

    It is not third. Cross out that color.

    It is not on the right. Cross out that color.

    It is not second. Cross out that color.

    Circle my sister's favorite color.

2. Circle the smaller number.

    29   23

3. Finish the repeating pattern.

    ○ , □ , □ , ○ , □ , □ , ___ , ___ , ___ , ___ , ___ , ___

4. What number is one more than **25**? _____

    What number is one less than **73**? _____

5. Find the number that belongs in the square with the **A**. _____

    Find the number that belongs in the square with the **B**. _____

    Fill in the missing numbers.

1	2			5					10
11								B	20
					27				
31									
41		A			46				50

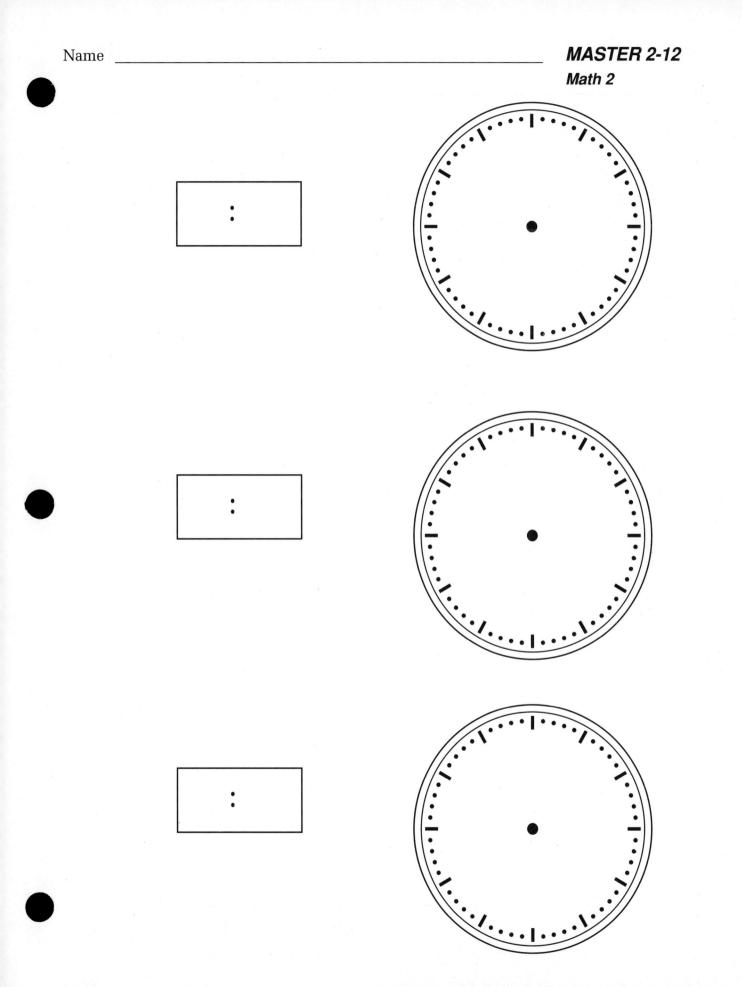

Name _____

A 2.0

```
    4        8        1        5        1
  + 1      + 1      + 2      + 1      + 7
  ———      ———      ———      ———      ———

    9        1        1        3        1
  + 1      + 1      + 6      + 1      + 9
  ———      ———      ———      ———      ———

    1        4        1        6        5
  + 3      + 1      + 0      + 1      + 1
  ———      ———      ———      ———      ———

    1        8        2        1        1
  + 5      + 1      + 1      + 7      + 1
  ———      ———      ———      ———      ———

    9        1        5        1        1
  + 1      + 6      + 1      + 0      + 1
  ———      ———      ———      ———      ———
```

Score: _____

2-12Fa

1. There were 10 children at the bus stop. Two more children joined them.

   What type of story is this?

   Circle one: Some, some more   Some, some went away

2. Circle the number that is one more than **31**.
   Draw a square around the number that is one less than **31**.

   28   29   31   30   32   27

3. Number the clock face.

   Show | **1:00** | on the clock.

4. Circle the squares that have equal size pieces.

5. Write these numbers using digits.

   thirty-seven _____   forty _____   sixteen _____

6. Find the answers.

   6 + 1 = _____   8 + 8 = _____   1 + 8 = _____   6 + 6 = _____

Name _____ **LESSON 12B**
                                                Math 2
Date _____

1. There were 10 children on the bus. One child got off the bus.

   What type of story is this?

   Circle one: Some, some more   Some, some went away

2. Circle the number that is one more than **26**.
   Draw a square around the number that is one less than **26**.

   27   29   26   24   28   25

3. Number the clock face.

   Show [**6:00**] on the clock.

4. Circle the circles that have equal size pieces.

5. Write these numbers.

   twenty-seven _____   eighty _____   thirteen _____

6. Find the answers.

   7 + 7 = _____   1 + 7 = _____   9 + 9 = _____   5 + 1 = _____

0	3	6	0	0
+ 7	+ 0	+ 0	+ 2	+ 0

9	0	3	0	5
+ 0	+ 6	+ 0	+ 8	+ 0

0	2	4	0	8
+ 1	+ 0	+ 0	+ 9	+ 0

7	0	6	0	1
+ 0	+ 5	+ 0	+ 0	+ 0

5	0	1	0	0
+ 0	+ 3	+ 0	+ 4	+ 9

Score: _____

Name _____

Date _____

1. How many children have birthdays in November? _____

    What is the third month of the year? _____

    How many children have birthdays in that month? _____

2. Circle the number that is one less than **24**.
    Draw a square around the number that is one more than **28**.

    25   34   22   27   23   29

3. One of these is my favorite bear.
    Use the clues to find my favorite
    bear.
        It is not on the left.
        It is not in the middle.
        It is not fourth.
        It is not second.
        Circle my favorite bear.

4. Number the clock face.

    Show | **2:00** | on the clock.

5. Finish the pattern.

    △, □, □, □, △, □, □, □, ____, ____, ____, ____,

Name _____

Date _____

1. Fill in the missing numbers.

    <u>21</u>, <u>22</u>, ___, ___, ___, ___, <u>27</u>, ___, ___, ___

    <u>31</u>, ___, ___, ___, ___, <u>36</u>, ___, ___, ___, ___

2. Circle the number that is one less than **37**.
   Draw a square around the number that is one more than **32**.

    38   33   39   34   31   36

3. One of these is my favorite bear.
   Use the clues to find my favorite
   bear.
    It is not on the left.
    It is not in the middle.
    It is not second.
    It is not the last.
    Circle my favorite bear.

4. Number the clock face.

    Show | **11:00** | on the clock.

5. Finish the pattern.

    ○ , △ , △ , □ , ○ , △ , △ , □ , ___ , ___ , ___ , ___

$$\begin{array}{r}4\\+\ 1\\\hline\end{array}\qquad\begin{array}{r}8\\+\ 1\\\hline\end{array}\qquad\begin{array}{r}1\\+\ 2\\\hline\end{array}\qquad\begin{array}{r}5\\+\ 1\\\hline\end{array}\qquad\begin{array}{r}1\\+\ 7\\\hline\end{array}$$

$$\begin{array}{r}9\\+\ 1\\\hline\end{array}\qquad\begin{array}{r}1\\+\ 1\\\hline\end{array}\qquad\begin{array}{r}1\\+\ 6\\\hline\end{array}\qquad\begin{array}{r}3\\+\ 1\\\hline\end{array}\qquad\begin{array}{r}1\\+\ 9\\\hline\end{array}$$

$$\begin{array}{r}1\\+\ 3\\\hline\end{array}\qquad\begin{array}{r}4\\+\ 1\\\hline\end{array}\qquad\begin{array}{r}1\\+\ 0\\\hline\end{array}\qquad\begin{array}{r}6\\+\ 1\\\hline\end{array}\qquad\begin{array}{r}5\\+\ 1\\\hline\end{array}$$

$$\begin{array}{r}1\\+\ 5\\\hline\end{array}\qquad\begin{array}{r}8\\+\ 1\\\hline\end{array}\qquad\begin{array}{r}2\\+\ 1\\\hline\end{array}\qquad\begin{array}{r}1\\+\ 7\\\hline\end{array}\qquad\begin{array}{r}1\\+\ 1\\\hline\end{array}$$

$$\begin{array}{r}9\\+\ 1\\\hline\end{array}\qquad\begin{array}{r}1\\+\ 6\\\hline\end{array}\qquad\begin{array}{r}5\\+\ 1\\\hline\end{array}\qquad\begin{array}{r}1\\+\ 0\\\hline\end{array}\qquad\begin{array}{r}1\\+\ 1\\\hline\end{array}$$

Score: _____

Name _____   **LESSON 14A**

Date _____   *Math 2*

1. Crystal's dog had seven puppies. She gave four of the puppies to friends.

    What type of story is this?

    Circle one: Some, some more   Some, some went away

2. Circle the fifth letter.
    Circle the twelfth letter.
    Circle the eighth letter.   O S P A E W A V O R E N
    Circle the eleventh letter.
    Circle the second letter.

3. Circle the smallest number.
    Put an X on the largest number.   27   15   24

4. Finish these repeating patterns.

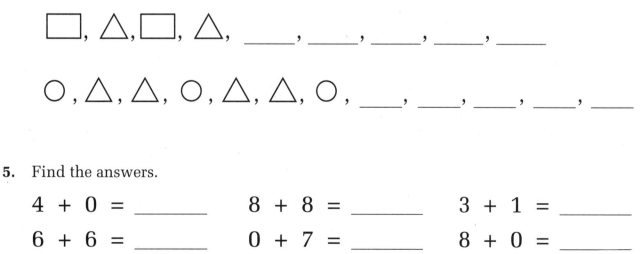

5. Find the answers.

    4 + 0 = _____   8 + 8 = _____   3 + 1 = _____

    6 + 6 = _____   0 + 7 = _____   8 + 0 = _____

    1 + 9 = _____   6 + 1 = _____   7 + 7 = _____

2-14Wa

Name _____   **LESSON 14B**
                                                    Math 2
Date _____

1. Carol had 17 pennies. She found 2 more pennies on the sidewalk.

    What type of story is this?

    Circle one: Some, some more   Some, some went away

2. Circle the fifth letter.
    Circle the twelfth letter.
    Circle the second letter.   S E N T I G A C H R E T
    Circle the ninth letter.
    Circle the sixth letter.

3. Circle the smallest number.
    Put an X on the largest number.   39   34   47

4. Finish these repeating patterns.

    △, □, △, □, ___, ___, ___, ___, ___

    □, □, ○, □, □, ○, □, ___, ___, ___, ___

5. Find the answers.

    5 + 5 = _____   8 + 1 = _____   9 + 0 = _____

    4 + 1 = _____   0 + 5 = _____   4 + 4 = _____

    0 + 6 = _____   9 + 9 = _____   1 + 5 = _____

1. Write a **K** in the fifth square.
   Write an **A** in the middle square.
   Write a **B** in the first square.
   Write a **C** in the fourth square.
   Write an **L** in the second square.

2. Circle the smaller number.

46	42

3. Count by 10's. Fill in the missing numbers.

   <u>10</u> ___ ___ ___ ___ ___ ___ ___ ___ ___

4. Fill in the missing numbers on the chart.

   What number belongs in the square with the **A**? _____

   What number belongs in the square with the **B**? _____

   What number belongs in the square with the **C**? _____

1			4						10
	12							C	
						A			30
		33		B					

5. Draw a square to the right of the triangle.
   Draw a circle to the left of the triangle.

6. Add.

   8 + 1 = _____   3 + 1 = _____   6 + 1 = _____   7 + 1 = _____

1 + 3	0 + 1	6 + 1	4 + 4	1 + 5
1 + 7	8 + 8	5 + 1	9 + 1	8 + 1
1 + 4	1 + 6	0 + 0	7 + 7	2 + 1
6 + 6	3 + 1	1 + 6	1 + 0	3 + 3
1 + 9	5 + 5	4 + 1	1 + 8	7 + 1

Score: _____

2-15Fa

Name _____

Date _____

1. Fill in the missing days of the week.

   Sunday, _____, _____, Wednesday,

   _____, _____, Saturday

2. Circle the weekdays in Problem 1.

3. Number the clock face.
   If it is 9:00 now, write the time one hour ago.
   Show this time on both clocks.

   ┌─────────────┐
   │   :   │
   └─────────────┘

4. What is one more than **39**? _____

   What is one less than **20**? _____

5. Write these letters in the squares below.

fourth square **H**	ninth square **F**	tenth square **U**
seventh square **S**	first square **M**	third square **T**
eleventh square **N**	sixth square **I**	second square **A**

   start
   here*   ☐ ☐ ☐ ☐ ☐ ☐ ☐ ☐ ☐ ☐ ☐ ☐

1. Fill in the missing days of the week.

   _____, Monday, Tuesday, _____,

   Thursday, Friday, _____

2. Circle the days of the weekend in Problem 1.

3. Number the clock face.
   If it is 2:00 now, write the time one hour ago.
   Show this time on both clocks.

   ┌─────────┐
   │   :   │
   └─────────┘

4. What is one more than **49**? _____

   What is one less than **40**? _____

5. Write these letters in the squares below.

   twelfth square **N**   eleventh square **O**   tenth square **O**
   fourth square **L**   ninth square **S**   third square **L**
   first square **C**   sixth square **M**   second square **A**
   seventh square **E**

   start
   here*   □ □ □ □ □ □ □ □ □ □ □ □

0 + 7	3 + 0	6 + 0	0 + 2	0 + 0
9 + 0	0 + 6	3 + 0	0 + 8	5 + 0
0 + 1	2 + 0	4 + 0	0 + 9	8 + 0
7 + 0	0 + 5	6 + 0	0 + 0	1 + 0
5 + 0	0 + 3	1 + 0	0 + 4	0 + 9

Score: _____

Name _____

Date _____

1. Dave had a set of 10 markers. His mother gave him another set of 10 markers.

   What type of story is this?

   Circle one: Some, some more   Some, some went away

2. Put an X on the circles that have equal size pieces.

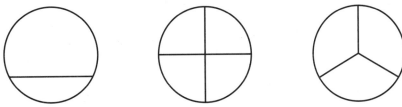

3. Color the graph to match your classroom graph.

   What day of the week is the favorite

   day? _____

   How many children chose Friday?

   _____

   Our Favorite Day of the Week

Sun	Mon	Tue	Wed	Thur	Fri	Sat

4. Circle the weekdays on the graph in Problem 3.

5. Write these numbers using digits.

   thirty-two _____   fourteen _____

6. Find the answers.

   $\begin{array}{r} 6 \\ +6 \\ \hline \end{array}$ $\begin{array}{r} 0 \\ +7 \\ \hline \end{array}$ $\begin{array}{r} 6 \\ +1 \\ \hline \end{array}$ $\begin{array}{r} 4 \\ +4 \\ \hline \end{array}$ $\begin{array}{r} 1 \\ +8 \\ \hline \end{array}$ $\begin{array}{r} 3 \\ +0 \\ \hline \end{array}$ $\begin{array}{r} 9 \\ +9 \\ \hline \end{array}$ $\begin{array}{r} 1 \\ +5 \\ \hline \end{array}$

Name _____

Date _____

1. Diane had 12 markers. She gave 2 markers to Frank.

    What type of story is this?

    Circle one: Some, some more   Some, some went away

2. Put an X on the circles that have equal size pieces.

    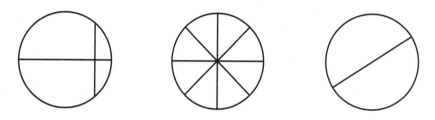

3. The children in Mrs. O'Neil's class made this graph.

    What day of the week is the children's

    favorite day? _____

    How many children chose Tuesday?

    _____

    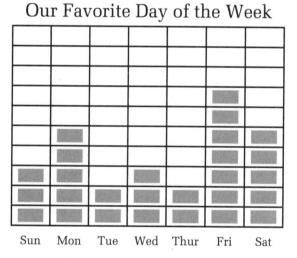

    Our Favorite Day of the Week

    Sun   Mon   Tue   Wed   Thur   Fri   Sat

4. Circle the weekend days on the graph in Problem 3.

5. Write these numbers using digits.

    forty-nine _____   seventeen _____

6. Find the answers.

$$\begin{array}{cccccccc} 5 & 8 & 0 & 3 & 7 & 8 & 8 & 1 \\ +0 & +8 & +9 & +3 & +1 & +8 & +0 & +4 \\ \hline \end{array}$$

1	2	3	4	5	6	7	8	9	10
11	12	13	14	15	16	17	18	19	20
21	22	23	24	25	26	27	28	29	30
31	32	33	34	35	36	37	38	39	40
41	42	43	44	45	46	47	48	49	50
51	52	53	54	55	56	57	58	59	60
61	62	63	64	65	66	67	68	69	70
71	72	73	74	75	76	77	78	79	80
81	82	83	84	85	86	87	88	89	90
91	92	93	94	95	96	97	98	99	100

Parents: This is a hundred number chart which we will use to examine number patterns. We will use this often during Math 2. Use this at home to help with homework assignments.

1 + 3	0 + 1	6 + 1	4 + 4	1 + 5
1 + 7	8 + 8	5 + 1	9 + 1	8 + 1
1 + 4	1 + 6	0 + 0	7 + 7	2 + 1
6 + 6	3 + 1	1 + 6	1 + 0	3 + 3
1 + 9	5 + 5	4 + 1	1 + 8	7 + 1

Score: _____

Name _____

Date _____

1. Use the Favorite Day of the Week graph to answer the questions.

   How many children like Friday best? _____

   How many children like Saturday best? _____

   Circle the day that more children chose: Friday   Saturday

   How many more children chose that day? _____

2. Fill in the missing days of the week.

   _____, Monday, Tuesday, Wednesday,

   _____, _____, _____

3. Circle the even numbers.

   1 , 2 , 3 , 4 , 5 , 6 , 7 , 8 , 9 , 10

   11 , 12 , 13 , 14 , 15 , 16 , 17 , 18 , 19 , 20

4. Circle the smallest number.   24   35   21

5. Number the clock face.
   If it is 4:00 now, write the time one hour from now.
   Show this time on both clocks.

   :

Name _____

Date _____

1. Fill in the missing days of the week.

   Sunday, _____, _____, Wednesday,

   _____, _____, Saturday

2. Circle the weekdays in Problem 1.

3. Circle the odd numbers.

   1 , 2 , 3 , 4 , 5 , 6 , 7 , 8 , 9 , 10

   11 , 12 , 13 , 14 , 15 , 16 , 17 , 18 , 19 , 20

4. Circle the smallest number.

37   21   35

5. Number the clock face.
   If it is 10:00 now, write the time one hour from now.
   Show this time on both clocks.

:

6. Which letter is sixth? _____

   Which letter is tenth? _____

   Which letter is fourth? _____

   Which letter is eleventh? _____

   M   T   A   L   O   H   B   X   N   E   P   S

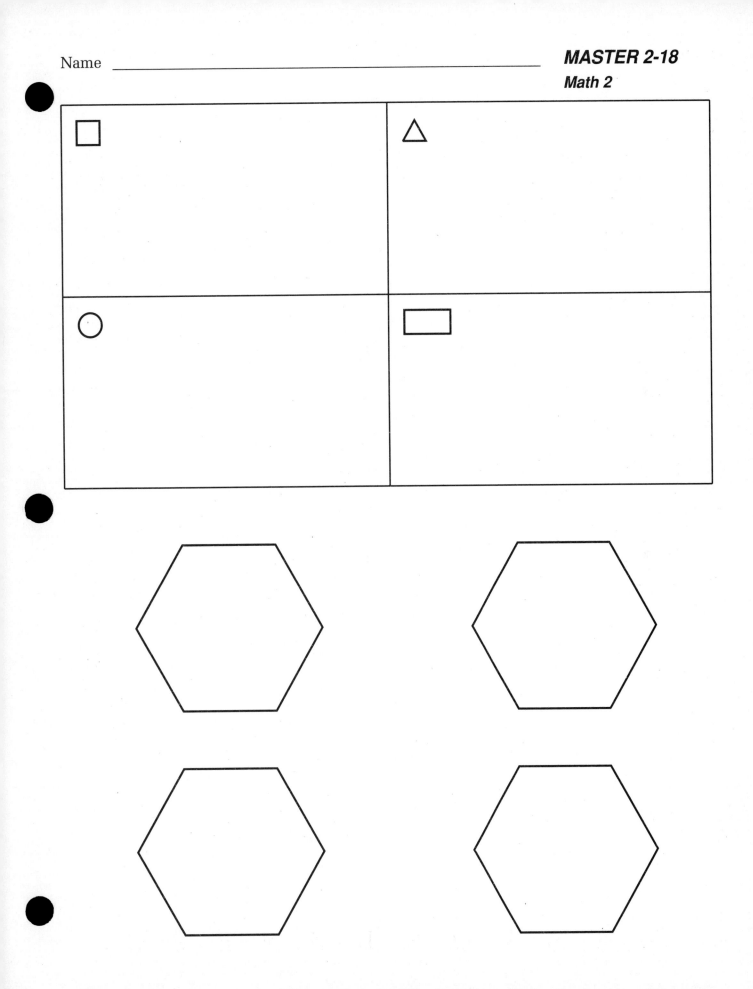

$$\begin{array}{r} 5 \\ +\,1 \\ \hline \end{array} \qquad \begin{array}{r} 3 \\ +\,3 \\ \hline \end{array} \qquad \begin{array}{r} 1 \\ +\,9 \\ \hline \end{array} \qquad \begin{array}{r} 4 \\ +\,4 \\ \hline \end{array} \qquad \begin{array}{r} 1 \\ +\,2 \\ \hline \end{array}$$

$$\begin{array}{r} 1 \\ +\,6 \\ \hline \end{array} \qquad \begin{array}{r} 0 \\ +\,9 \\ \hline \end{array} \qquad \begin{array}{r} 7 \\ +\,7 \\ \hline \end{array} \qquad \begin{array}{r} 5 \\ +\,0 \\ \hline \end{array} \qquad \begin{array}{r} 9 \\ +\,9 \\ \hline \end{array}$$

$$\begin{array}{r} 9 \\ +\,1 \\ \hline \end{array} \qquad \begin{array}{r} 0 \\ +\,7 \\ \hline \end{array} \qquad \begin{array}{r} 3 \\ +\,1 \\ \hline \end{array} \qquad \begin{array}{r} 4 \\ +\,4 \\ \hline \end{array} \qquad \begin{array}{r} 1 \\ +\,8 \\ \hline \end{array}$$

$$\begin{array}{r} 4 \\ +\,0 \\ \hline \end{array} \qquad \begin{array}{r} 7 \\ +\,7 \\ \hline \end{array} \qquad \begin{array}{r} 2 \\ +\,2 \\ \hline \end{array} \qquad \begin{array}{r} 1 \\ +\,7 \\ \hline \end{array} \qquad \begin{array}{r} 8 \\ +\,0 \\ \hline \end{array}$$

$$\begin{array}{r} 5 \\ +\,5 \\ \hline \end{array} \qquad \begin{array}{r} 8 \\ +\,8 \\ \hline \end{array} \qquad \begin{array}{r} 0 \\ +\,6 \\ \hline \end{array} \qquad \begin{array}{r} 6 \\ +\,6 \\ \hline \end{array} \qquad \begin{array}{r} 1 \\ +\,4 \\ \hline \end{array}$$

Score: _____

Name _____

● Date _____

1. Fran read 6 pages in her book before dinner. After dinner she read 6 more pages.

    What type of story is this?

    Circle one: Some, some more   Some, some went away

2. Use the Favorite Day of the Week graph to answer the questions.

    How many children chose Sunday? _____

    How many more children chose Saturday than chose Monday? _____

3. Use ○ and △ to make a repeating pattern.

    ____, ____, ____, ____, ____, ____, ____, ____, ____, ____, ____, ____

4. Color the sixth shape in Problem 3 red.
    Color the eleventh shape in Problem 3 green.
    Color the ninth shape in Problem 3 blue.

5. Write these numbers using digits.

    thirty-one _____   thirteen _____

6. Color the triangle green.
    Color the square orange.
    Color the circle blue.
    Color the rectangle yellow.

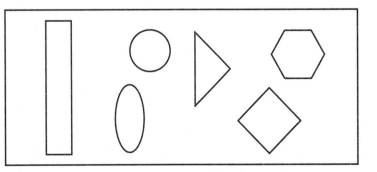

1. Mary brought 6 crackers to school. She ate two at lunch.

    What type of story is this?

    Circle one: Some, some more   Some, some went away

2. Circle the squares that have equal size pieces.

3. Use △ and ☐ to make a repeating pattern.

    ____, ____, ____, ____, ____, ____, ____, ____, ____, ____, ____, ____

4. Color the seventh shape in Problem 3 orange.
    Color the tenth shape in Problem 3 yellow.
    Color the fifth shape in Problem 3 brown.

5. Write these numbers using digits.

    sixteen _____   sixty-one _____

6. Color the triangle green.
    Color the square orange.
    Color the circle blue.
    Color the rectangle yellow.

5 + 1	3 + 3	1 + 9	4 + 4	1 + 2
1 + 6	0 + 9	7 + 7	5 + 0	9 + 9
9 + 1	0 + 7	3 + 1	4 + 4	1 + 8
4 + 0	7 + 7	2 + 2	1 + 7	8 + 0
5 + 5	8 + 8	0 + 6	6 + 6	1 + 4

Score: _____

1. Fill in the missing days of the week.

   Sunday, _____, _____, _____,

   Thursday, _____, _____

2. Match each name with the correct piece.

   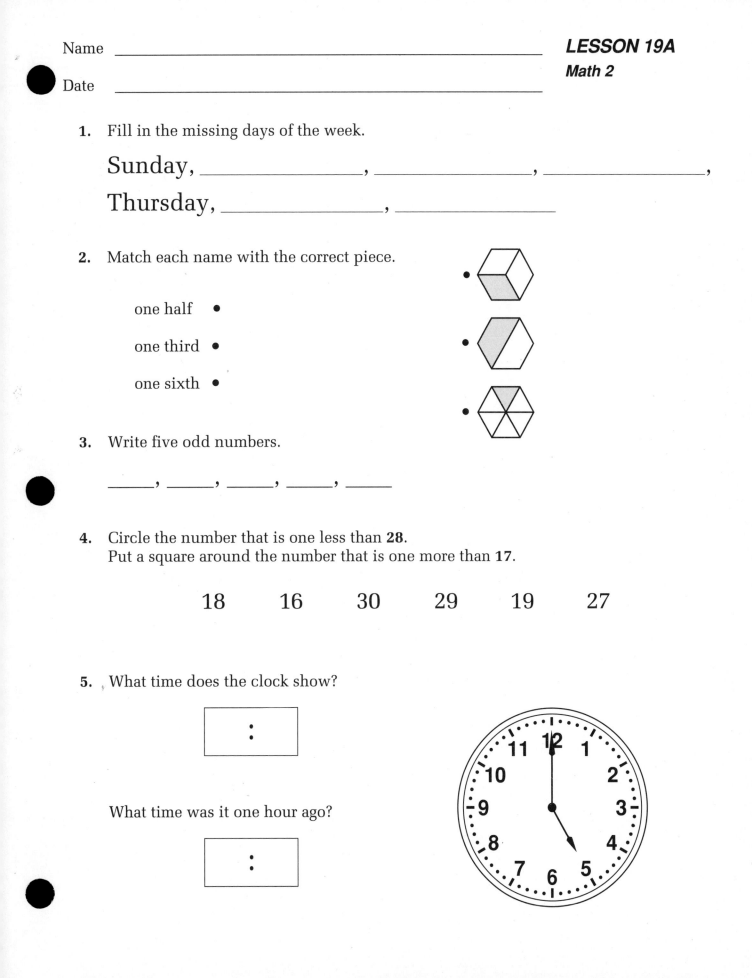

   one half •

   one third •

   one sixth •

3. Write five odd numbers.

   _____, _____, _____, _____, _____

4. Circle the number that is one less than **28**.
   Put a square around the number that is one more than **17**.

   18   16   30   29   19   27

5. What time does the clock show?

   [:]

   What time was it one hour ago?

   [:]

Name _____

Date _____

1. Fill in the missing numbers on this piece of a hundred number chart.

41	42	43	44						50
51					56				
									70
71									

What number is to the right of **56**? _____

What number is to the left of **56**? _____

What number is above **56**? _____

What number is below **56**? _____

2. Write five even numbers.

_____, _____, _____, _____, _____

3. Circle the number that is one less than **42**.
   Put a square around the number that is one more than **23**.

   41   21   24   43   44   22

4. What time does the clock show?

What time was it one hour ago?

Name _____

ASSESSMENT 3
LESSON 20
Math 2

Date _____

1. John has 8 pennies. Susan gave him 2 pennies. How many pennies does John have now?

   What type of story is this?

   Circle one: some, some more   some, some went away

   Four children were playing. One child went home. How many children are playing now?

   What type of story is this?

   Circle one: some, some more   some, some went away

2. Finish the repeating pattern.

   △, ○, ○, □, △, ○, ○, □, △, ____ , ____ , ____ , ____

3. Write these numbers using digits.

   fourteen _____   thirty-five _____

   sixty-one _____   seventy _____

4. Circle the shapes that have equal size pieces.

5. What is one more than **49**? _____

   What is one less than **20**? _____

6. Add.

   6 + 1 = _____   5 + 0 = _____   8 + 8 = _____   0 + 7 = _____

   7 + 7 = _____   1 + 8 = _____   3 + 3 = _____   9 + 9 = _____

2-20Aa

Copyright by Saxon Publishers, Inc. and Nancy Larson. Reproduction prohibited.

Name _____

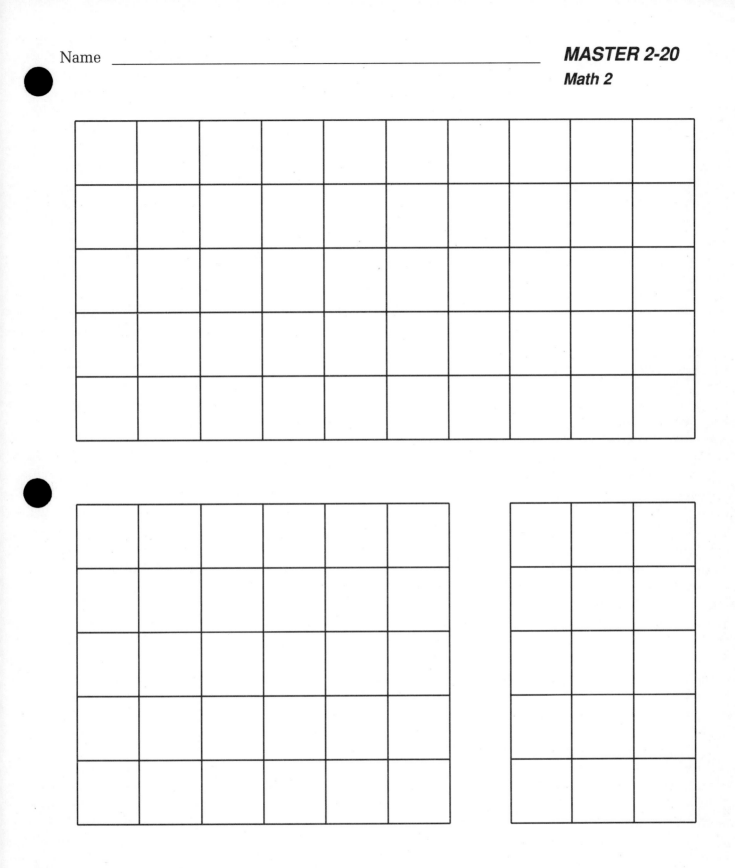

Name _____

A 3.2

$$\begin{array}{r}5\\+1\\\hline\end{array}\quad\begin{array}{r}3\\+3\\\hline\end{array}\quad\begin{array}{r}1\\+9\\\hline\end{array}\quad\begin{array}{r}4\\+4\\\hline\end{array}\quad\begin{array}{r}1\\+2\\\hline\end{array}$$

$$\begin{array}{r}1\\+6\\\hline\end{array}\quad\begin{array}{r}0\\+9\\\hline\end{array}\quad\begin{array}{r}7\\+7\\\hline\end{array}\quad\begin{array}{r}5\\+0\\\hline\end{array}\quad\begin{array}{r}9\\+9\\\hline\end{array}$$

$$\begin{array}{r}9\\+1\\\hline\end{array}\quad\begin{array}{r}0\\+7\\\hline\end{array}\quad\begin{array}{r}3\\+1\\\hline\end{array}\quad\begin{array}{r}4\\+4\\\hline\end{array}\quad\begin{array}{r}1\\+8\\\hline\end{array}$$

$$\begin{array}{r}4\\+0\\\hline\end{array}\quad\begin{array}{r}7\\+7\\\hline\end{array}\quad\begin{array}{r}2\\+2\\\hline\end{array}\quad\begin{array}{r}1\\+7\\\hline\end{array}\quad\begin{array}{r}8\\+0\\\hline\end{array}$$

$$\begin{array}{r}5\\+5\\\hline\end{array}\quad\begin{array}{r}8\\+8\\\hline\end{array}\quad\begin{array}{r}0\\+6\\\hline\end{array}\quad\begin{array}{r}6\\+6\\\hline\end{array}\quad\begin{array}{r}1\\+4\\\hline\end{array}$$

Score: _____

2-20Fa

Name _____

3 + 2	1 + 2	6 + 2	2 + 2	9 + 2
0 + 2	8 + 2	2 + 2	5 + 2	4 + 2
1 + 2	5 + 2	4 + 2	7 + 2	3 + 2
9 + 2	6 + 2	4 + 2	0 + 2	8 + 2
9 + 2	3 + 2	5 + 2	6 + 2	1 + 2

Score: _____

Name _____ **LESSON 21A**

Date _____ *Math 2*

1. There are 12 girls in Mrs. Miller's class. There are 10 boys in Mrs. Miller's class.

    What type of story is this?

    Circle one: some, some more   some, some went away

2. Color one half red.   Color one third blue.   Color one sixth green.

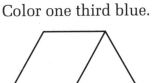

3. Write these numbers using digits.

    fifty-nine _____   ninety-five _____

4. Finish the repeating pattern.
    Color the pattern: (R = Red, B = Blue, G = Green)

    | R | B | B | G | R | B | B | G | | | | | | | | | |

5. Find the answers.

    6 + 2 = _____   9 + 2 = _____   4 + 2 = _____

6. Color all the squares orange.
    Color all the circles yellow.
    Color all the triangles green.
    Color all the rectangles red.

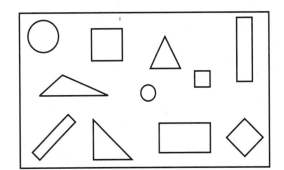

Name _____   **LESSON 21B**
                                                           Math 2
Date _____

1. There were twenty-five children in Mrs. Butler's class. Two children went to the gym.

   What type of story is this?

   Circle one: some, some more   some, some went away

2. Color one half red.   Color one third blue.   Color one sixth green.

3. Write these numbers using digits.

   seventy-eight _____   eighty-seven _____

4. Finish the repeating pattern.
   Color the pattern: (R = Red, B = Blue, G = Green)

   | G | B | R | R | G | B | R | R | | | | | | | | | |

5. Find the answers.

   8 + 2 = _____   5 + 2 = _____   3 + 2 = _____

6. Color all the squares orange.
   Color all the circles yellow.
   Color all the triangles green.
   Color all the rectangles red.

Name _____

A 3.2

$$\begin{array}{r} 5 \\ +\ 1 \\ \hline \end{array} \quad \begin{array}{r} 3 \\ +\ 3 \\ \hline \end{array} \quad \begin{array}{r} 1 \\ +\ 9 \\ \hline \end{array} \quad \begin{array}{r} 4 \\ +\ 4 \\ \hline \end{array} \quad \begin{array}{r} 1 \\ +\ 2 \\ \hline \end{array}$$

$$\begin{array}{r} 1 \\ +\ 6 \\ \hline \end{array} \quad \begin{array}{r} 0 \\ +\ 9 \\ \hline \end{array} \quad \begin{array}{r} 7 \\ +\ 7 \\ \hline \end{array} \quad \begin{array}{r} 5 \\ +\ 0 \\ \hline \end{array} \quad \begin{array}{r} 9 \\ +\ 9 \\ \hline \end{array}$$

$$\begin{array}{r} 9 \\ +\ 1 \\ \hline \end{array} \quad \begin{array}{r} 0 \\ +\ 7 \\ \hline \end{array} \quad \begin{array}{r} 3 \\ +\ 1 \\ \hline \end{array} \quad \begin{array}{r} 4 \\ +\ 4 \\ \hline \end{array} \quad \begin{array}{r} 1 \\ +\ 8 \\ \hline \end{array}$$

$$\begin{array}{r} 4 \\ +\ 0 \\ \hline \end{array} \quad \begin{array}{r} 7 \\ +\ 7 \\ \hline \end{array} \quad \begin{array}{r} 2 \\ +\ 2 \\ \hline \end{array} \quad \begin{array}{r} 1 \\ +\ 7 \\ \hline \end{array} \quad \begin{array}{r} 8 \\ +\ 0 \\ \hline \end{array}$$

$$\begin{array}{r} 5 \\ +\ 5 \\ \hline \end{array} \quad \begin{array}{r} 8 \\ +\ 8 \\ \hline \end{array} \quad \begin{array}{r} 0 \\ +\ 6 \\ \hline \end{array} \quad \begin{array}{r} 6 \\ +\ 6 \\ \hline \end{array} \quad \begin{array}{r} 1 \\ +\ 4 \\ \hline \end{array}$$

Score: _____

2-22Fa

Name _____

Date _____

1. Use the Favorite Day of the Week graph to answer the questions.

   How many children chose a weekday as their favorite day? _____

   How many children chose a day of the weekend as their favorite day? _____

2. Write the even numbers from 2 to 20.

   __2__ , ___ , ___ , ___ , ___ , ___ , ___ , ___ , ___ , __20__

   Write the odd numbers from 1 to 19.

   __1__ , ___ , ___ , ___ , ___ , ___ , ___ , ___ , ___ , __19__

3. Circle the greatest number.

   | 47 | 43 | 49 |

4. How are these shapes the same?

   _____

   _____

5. Number the clock face.

   If it is 12:00 now, write the digital time one hour ago.

   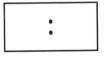

   Show this time on the clock face.

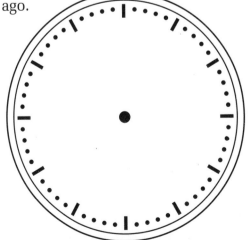

2-22Wa

Name _____

Date _____

1. Fill in the missing numbers on this piece of a hundred number chart.

61									70
71			74						80
81									90

What number is to the right of 74? _____   What number is to the left of 74? _____

What number is above 74? _____   What number is below 74? _____

2. Write the even numbers from 20 to 2.

   <u>20</u> , <u>18</u> , <u>16</u> , <u>14</u> , ___ , ___ , ___ , ___ , ___ , <u>2</u>

   Write the odd numbers from 19 to 1.

   <u>19</u> , <u>17</u> , <u>15</u> , <u>13</u> , ___ , ___ , ___ , ___ , ___ , <u>1</u>

3. Circle the greatest number.

   36   34   33

4. How are these shapes different?

   _____

   _____

5. Number the clock face.

   If it is 6:00 now, write the digital time one hour ago.

   [__ : __]

   Show this time on the clock face.

3	1	6	2	2
+ 2	+ 2	+ 2	+ 2	+ 9

0	8	2	5	4
+ 2	+ 2	+ 2	+ 2	+ 2

1	5	4	7	3
+ 2	+ 2	+ 2	+ 2	+ 2

9	6	4	0	8
+ 2	+ 2	+ 2	+ 2	+ 2

9	3	5	6	1
+ 2	+ 2	+ 2	+ 2	+ 2

Score: _____

2-23Fa

Name _____

Date _____

LESSON 23A
Math 2

Draw a picture and write a number sentence for each story. Write the answer with a label.

1. Susan has two new pencils and three old pencils. How many pencils does she have?

Number sentence _____

Answer _____

2. Steven had 10 markers. He gave 3 markers to his friend. How many markers does he have now?

Number sentence _____

Answer _____

3. Write the names of the weekdays.

_____

_____

4. Match each name with the correct piece.

one half •

one sixth •

one third •

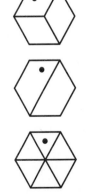

2-23Wa

Name _____ **LESSON 23B**

Date _____ *Math 2* ●

Draw a picture and write a number sentence for each story. Write the answer with a label.

1. Sharon's mom bought four blueberry muffins and three apple muffins at the store. How many muffins did she buy?

   [ ]

   Number sentence _____

   Answer _____

2. There were 12 eggs in the carton. Scott's family ate 5 eggs for breakfast. How many eggs are left in the carton now?

   [ ] ●

   Number sentence _____

   Answer _____

3. Circle the names of the days of the weekend.

   Sunday, Monday, Tuesday, Wednesday, Thursday, Friday, Saturday

4. Ask the members of your family what their favorite days of the week are. Write each person's name under the day they chose in Problem 3.

5. Find something at home that has the shape of a rectangle and something that has the shape of a triangle. Draw pictures of what you found.

rectangle	triangle

   ●

Name _____

$$
\begin{array}{r} 2 \\ +\ 3 \\ \hline \end{array}
\qquad
\begin{array}{r} 8 \\ +\ 2 \\ \hline \end{array}
\qquad
\begin{array}{r} 2 \\ +\ 7 \\ \hline \end{array}
\qquad
\begin{array}{r} 4 \\ +\ 2 \\ \hline \end{array}
\qquad
\begin{array}{r} 9 \\ +\ 2 \\ \hline \end{array}
$$

$$
\begin{array}{r} 2 \\ +\ 5 \\ \hline \end{array}
\qquad
\begin{array}{r} 2 \\ +\ 9 \\ \hline \end{array}
\qquad
\begin{array}{r} 3 \\ +\ 2 \\ \hline \end{array}
\qquad
\begin{array}{r} 6 \\ +\ 2 \\ \hline \end{array}
\qquad
\begin{array}{r} 2 \\ +\ 8 \\ \hline \end{array}
$$

$$
\begin{array}{r} 2 \\ +\ 4 \\ \hline \end{array}
\qquad
\begin{array}{r} 7 \\ +\ 2 \\ \hline \end{array}
\qquad
\begin{array}{r} 2 \\ +\ 6 \\ \hline \end{array}
\qquad
\begin{array}{r} 9 \\ +\ 2 \\ \hline \end{array}
\qquad
\begin{array}{r} 5 \\ +\ 2 \\ \hline \end{array}
$$

$$
\begin{array}{r} 2 \\ +\ 7 \\ \hline \end{array}
\qquad
\begin{array}{r} 2 \\ +\ 3 \\ \hline \end{array}
\qquad
\begin{array}{r} 2 \\ +\ 6 \\ \hline \end{array}
\qquad
\begin{array}{r} 8 \\ +\ 2 \\ \hline \end{array}
\qquad
\begin{array}{r} 2 \\ +\ 5 \\ \hline \end{array}
$$

$$
\begin{array}{r} 6 \\ +\ 2 \\ \hline \end{array}
\qquad
\begin{array}{r} 2 \\ +\ 9 \\ \hline \end{array}
\qquad
\begin{array}{r} 4 \\ +\ 2 \\ \hline \end{array}
\qquad
\begin{array}{r} 2 \\ +\ 8 \\ \hline \end{array}
\qquad
\begin{array}{r} 7 \\ +\ 2 \\ \hline \end{array}
$$

Score: _____

Name _____

Date _____

Draw a picture and write a number sentence for each story. Write the answer with a label.

1. There were 4 plants in Room 2. The children brought in 3 more. How many plants are in the room now?

   [ ]

   Number sentence _____

   Answer _____

2. Melanie bought five lunch tickets. She used two. How many tickets does she have now?

   [ ]

   Number sentence _____

   Answer _____

3. Number the clock face.

   If it is 5:00 now, write the digital time one hour from now.

   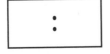

   Show this time on the clock face.

   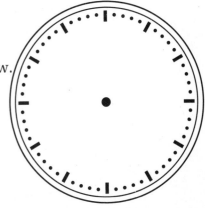

4. Draw a line to divide each shape in half.
   Shade one half.

   [ ]   [ ]

Name _____   **LESSON 24B**

Date _____   *Math 2*

Draw a picture and write a number sentence for each story. Write the answer with a label.

1. There were 7 fish in Room 5's fish tank. Mrs. Weber put 2 more fish in the tank. How many fish are in the tank now?

    Number sentence _____

    Answer _____

2. There were five birds at the bird feeder. Three flew away. How many birds are at the feeder now?

    Number sentence _____

    Answer _____

3. Number the clock face.

    If it is 6:00 now, write the digital time one hour from now.

    [:   ]

    Show this time on the clock face.

4. Draw a line to divide each shape in half.
    Shade one half.

1. Use the Favorite Day of the Week graph to answer these questions.

   What day of the week did the most children choose? _____

   How many children chose the first day of the week as their favorite day? _____

   How many more children chose Saturday than chose Wednesday? _____

2. Write the names of the weekdays. You may use the calendar to help you spell the names of the days.

   _____

   _____

3. Write these letters in the squares below.

   sixth square E   tenth square I   eighth square S   ninth square M
   first square S   third square E   twelfth square E   eleventh square L
   fifth square M   second square E

   ☐ ☐ ☐ ☐ ☐ ☐ ☐ ☐ ☐ ☐ ☐ ☐

4. Circle the even numbers.

   17   6   20   5   14   8

5. Number the clock face. If it is two o'clock now, write the time one hour from now. Show this time on both clocks.

   [:]

6. Color the triangle green.
   Color the square orange.
   Color the circle yellow.
   Color the rectangle blue.

   ○   △   ☐   ▭

2 + 3	8 + 2	2 + 7	4 + 2	9 + 2
2 + 5	2 + 9	3 + 2	6 + 2	2 + 8
2 + 4	7 + 2	2 + 6	9 + 2	5 + 2
2 + 7	2 + 3	2 + 6	8 + 2	2 + 5
6 + 2	2 + 9	4 + 2	2 + 8	7 + 2

Score: _____

Name _____

Date _____

Draw a picture and write a number sentence for this story. Write the answer with a label.

1. Four girls were playing at the playground. Stephanie joined them. How many girls are playing now?

   ┌───┐
   │   │
   │   │
   │   │
   │   │
   └───┘

   Number sentence _____

   Answer _____

2. Circle the even numbers.

   14   7   9   8   4   18   6   3

3. Write the names for the first four months.

   _____, _____, _____, _____

4. Show two different ways to divide a square in half.

   ┌──────────┐   ┌──────────┐
   │   │   │   │
   │   │   │   │
   └──────────┘   └──────────┘

5. Number the clock face.

   Show half past three.

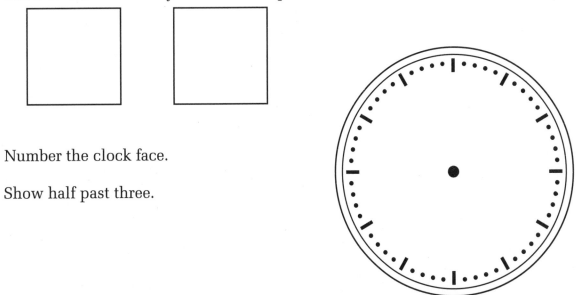

Name _____

Date _____

Draw a picture and write a number sentence for this story. Write the answer with a label.

1. At the first bus stop, four children got on the bus. At the next stop, three children got on the bus. How many children are on the bus now?

   Number sentence _____

   Answer _____

2. Circle the odd numbers.

   14   7   9   8   4   18   6   3

3. What month comes just before April? _____

   What month comes just after January? _____

4. Divide each shape in half. Shade one half.

5. Number the clock face.

   Show half past eight.

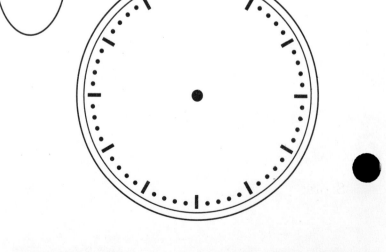

2 + 3	8 + 2	2 + 7	4 + 2	9 + 2
2 + 5	2 + 9	3 + 2	6 + 2	2 + 8
2 + 4	7 + 2	2 + 6	9 + 2	5 + 2
2 + 7	2 + 3	2 + 6	8 + 2	2 + 5
6 + 2	2 + 9	4 + 2	2 + 8	7 + 2

Score: _____

Draw a picture and write a number sentence for this story.

1. There are four green lunch boxes and three yellow lunch boxes on the shelf in Mr. Taylor's room. There are two green lunch boxes on the floor. How many green lunch boxes are there altogether?

Number sentence _____

Answer _____

2. Write the 10's on the thermometer.
   Which number on the thermometer

   is the temperature closest to? _____ °F

3. Finish the repeating pattern.
   Color the pattern. (R = Red, G = Green, Y = Yellow)

   | R | G | Y | G | R | G | Y | G | | | | | | | | |

4. Divide the squares in half two different ways.

   Color one half of each square red.

5. Change these doubles examples into doubles plus one examples.

$$\begin{array}{r}4\\+\,4\\\hline 8\end{array} \quad +\underline{} \qquad \begin{array}{r}7\\+\,7\\\hline 14\end{array} \quad +\underline{} \qquad \begin{array}{r}5\\+\,5\\\hline 10\end{array} \quad +\underline{}$$

0°

−10°

−20°

Name _____

Date _____

Math 2

●

Draw a picture and write a number sentence for this story.

1. Maureen put four cartons of grape juice and three cartons of apple juice on the table. There are two cartons of apple juice in the refrigerator. How many cartons of apple juice does Maureen have?

┌───┐
│   │
│   │
│   │
└───┘

   Number sentence _____

   Answer _____

2. Write the 10's on the thermometer.
   Which number on the thermometer

   is the temperature closest to? _____ °F

3. Finish the repeating pattern.
   Color the pattern. (R = Red, G = Green, Y = Yellow)

   | R | R | Y | G | G | R | R | Y | G | G | | | | | |

4. Divide the squares in half two different ways.

   ┌──────────┐   ┌──────────┐
   │   │   │   │
   │   │   │   │
   │   │   │   │
   └──────────┘   └──────────┘

   Color one half of each square red.

5. Change these doubles examples into doubles plus one examples.

   $\begin{array}{r} 3 \\ +\ 3 \\ \hline 6 \end{array}$ $+\ \underline{}$

   $\begin{array}{r} 8 \\ +\ 8 \\ \hline 16 \end{array}$ $+\ \underline{}$

   $\begin{array}{r} 6 \\ +\ 6 \\ \hline 12 \end{array}$ $+\ \underline{}$

0°

−10°

−20°

●

Name _____

5	8	2		9	5	7		6	4	7
+4	+1	+7		+0	+2	+8		+2	+3	+7

$$
\begin{array}{cc}
5 & 5 \\
+5 & +6 \\
\end{array}
\qquad
\begin{array}{cc}
7 & 8 \\
+7 & +7 \\
\end{array}
\qquad
\begin{array}{cc}
4 & 5 \\
+4 & +4 \\
\end{array}
$$

$$
\begin{array}{cc}
3 & 4 \\
+3 & +3 \\
\end{array}
\qquad
\begin{array}{cc}
6 & 6 \\
+6 & +7 \\
\end{array}
\qquad
\begin{array}{cc}
8 & 8 \\
+8 & +9 \\
\end{array}
$$

$$
\begin{array}{cc}
2 & 2 \\
+2 & +3 \\
\end{array}
\qquad
\begin{array}{cc}
5 & 6 \\
+5 & +5 \\
\end{array}
\qquad
\begin{array}{cc}
6 & 7 \\
+6 & +6 \\
\end{array}
$$

$$
\begin{array}{cc}
8 & 9 \\
+8 & +8 \\
\end{array}
\qquad
\begin{array}{cc}
3 & 3 \\
+3 & +4 \\
\end{array}
\qquad
\begin{array}{cc}
7 & 7 \\
+7 & +8 \\
\end{array}
$$

Name _____

A 5.1

3 + 4	6 + 7	9 + 8	5 + 4	7 + 8
6 + 5	8 + 9	4 + 3	7 + 6	4 + 5
8 + 7	3 + 4	5 + 4	9 + 8	5 + 6
6 + 7	4 + 5	7 + 8	6 + 5	8 + 9
3 + 4	7 + 6	5 + 6	9 + 8	8 + 7

Score: _____

2-27Fa

Name _____

● Date _____

Draw a picture and write a number sentence for this story. Write the answer with a label.

1. There were ten apples in a basket. Seth ate three apples. How many apples are in the basket now?

[blank box]

   Number sentence _____

   Answer _____

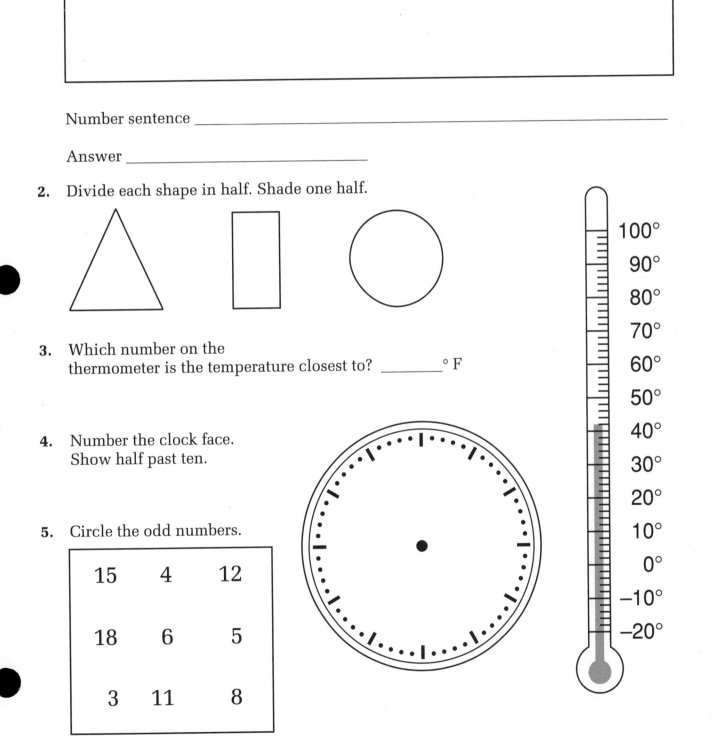

2. Divide each shape in half. Shade one half.

3. Which number on the thermometer is the temperature closest to? _____° F

4. Number the clock face. Show half past ten.

5. Circle the odd numbers.

15	4	12
18	6	5
3	11	8

Name _____

Date _____

Draw a picture and write a number sentence for this story. Write the answer with a label.

1. There were seven flies in the room. Two flew out the window. How many flies are in the room now?

    [blank box]

    Number sentence _____

    Answer _____

2. Divide each shape in half. Shade one half.

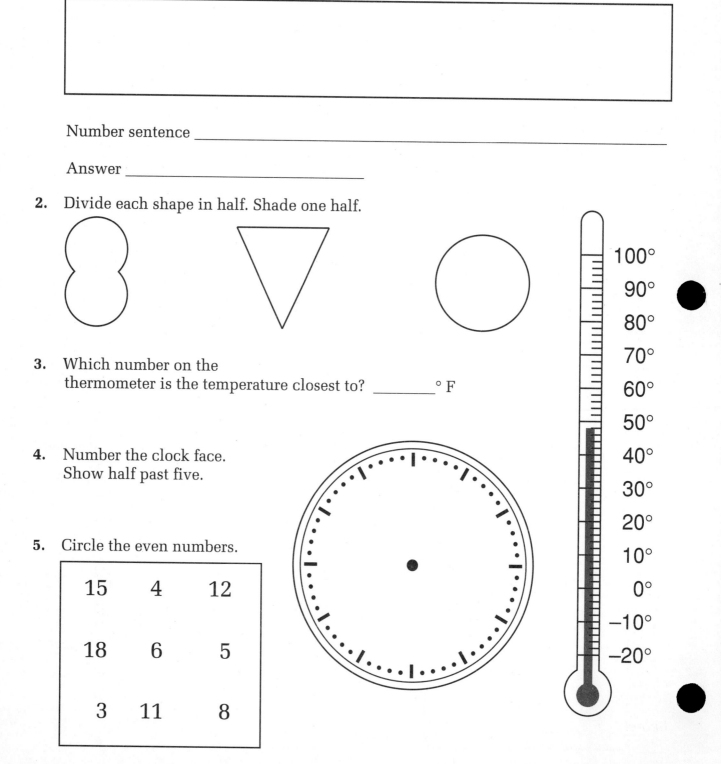

3. Which number on the
    thermometer is the temperature closest to? _____° F

4. Number the clock face.
    Show half past five.

5. Circle the even numbers.

15	4	12
18	6	5
3	11	8

2 + 0	2 + 6	3 + 3	1 + 9	2 + 2
7 + 7	1 + 3	9 + 9	0 + 3	1 + 1
0 + 9	4 + 4	1 + 6	4 + 2	6 + 6
7 + 1	5 + 5	8 + 0	6 + 6	5 + 1
8 + 8	2 + 7	3 + 2	8 + 1	2 + 8

Score: _____

2-28Fa

Name _____

Date _____

Draw a picture and write a number sentence for this story. Write the answer with a label.

1. Lee and Gail are having a party. Six friends are coming to the party. How many children will be at the party?

[ ]

Number sentence _____

Answer _____

2. Count by 10's. Write the numbers.

   _10_ , ___ , ___ , ___ , ___ , ___ , ___ , ___ , ___ , ___

3. How much money is this? _____

4. Which number on the thermometer is the temperature closest to? _____° F

5. How are these shapes the same? [ ] [ ]

   _____

   _____

6. Finish the pattern.

   △, □, ○, △, □, ○, △, ___, ___, ___, ___, ___

100°
90°
80°
70°
60°
50°
40°
30°
20°
10°
0°
−10°
−20°

Name _____

Date _____

Draw a picture and write a number sentence for this story. Write the answer with a label.

1. Marsha and Susan went to the movies with three friends. How many children went to the movies together?

    ┌───┐
    │   │
    │   │
    │   │
    │   │
    └───┘

    Number sentence _____

    Answer _____

2. Count backward by 10's. Write the numbers.

    100, _____, _____, _____, _____, _____, _____, _____, _____, _____

3. How much money is this? _____

4. Which number on the thermometer is the temperature closest to? _____ ° F

5. How are these shapes different?   ☐   ☐

    _____

    _____

6. What time (to the nearest half hour) do you usually wake up on a school day?

    ┌──────────┐
    │   │
    │   │
    └──────────┘

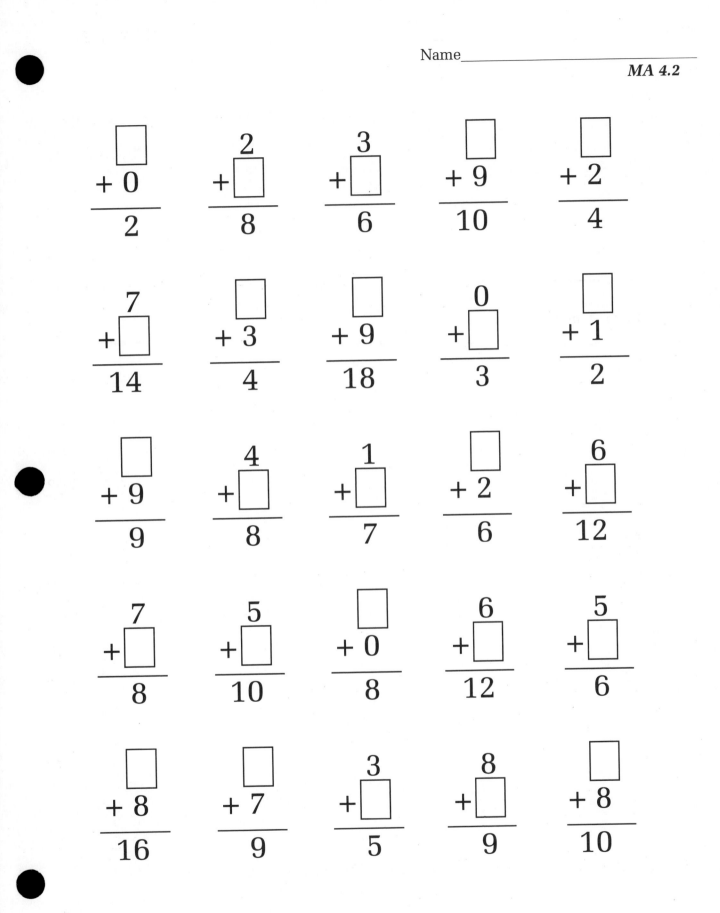

$$\begin{array}{r}\square \\ +\ 0 \\ \hline 2\end{array}\qquad\begin{array}{r}2 \\ +\ \square \\ \hline 8\end{array}\qquad\begin{array}{r}3 \\ +\ \square \\ \hline 6\end{array}\qquad\begin{array}{r}\square \\ +\ 9 \\ \hline 10\end{array}\qquad\begin{array}{r}\square \\ +\ 2 \\ \hline 4\end{array}$$

$$\begin{array}{r}7 \\ +\ \square \\ \hline 14\end{array}\qquad\begin{array}{r}\square \\ +\ 3 \\ \hline 4\end{array}\qquad\begin{array}{r}\square \\ +\ 9 \\ \hline 18\end{array}\qquad\begin{array}{r}0 \\ +\ \square \\ \hline 3\end{array}\qquad\begin{array}{r}\square \\ +\ 1 \\ \hline 2\end{array}$$

$$\begin{array}{r}\square \\ +\ 9 \\ \hline 9\end{array}\qquad\begin{array}{r}4 \\ +\ \square \\ \hline 8\end{array}\qquad\begin{array}{r}1 \\ +\ \square \\ \hline 7\end{array}\qquad\begin{array}{r}\square \\ +\ 2 \\ \hline 6\end{array}\qquad\begin{array}{r}6 \\ +\ \square \\ \hline 12\end{array}$$

$$\begin{array}{r}7 \\ +\ \square \\ \hline 8\end{array}\qquad\begin{array}{r}5 \\ +\ \square \\ \hline 10\end{array}\qquad\begin{array}{r}\square \\ +\ 0 \\ \hline 8\end{array}\qquad\begin{array}{r}6 \\ +\ \square \\ \hline 12\end{array}\qquad\begin{array}{r}5 \\ +\ \square \\ \hline 6\end{array}$$

$$\begin{array}{r}\square \\ +\ 8 \\ \hline 16\end{array}\qquad\begin{array}{r}\square \\ +\ 7 \\ \hline 9\end{array}\qquad\begin{array}{r}3 \\ +\ \square \\ \hline 5\end{array}\qquad\begin{array}{r}8 \\ +\ \square \\ \hline 9\end{array}\qquad\begin{array}{r}\square \\ +\ 8 \\ \hline 10\end{array}$$

Score:_____

$$\begin{array}{r} 2 \\ + 0 \\ \hline \end{array} \qquad \begin{array}{r} 2 \\ + 6 \\ \hline \end{array} \qquad \begin{array}{r} 3 \\ + 3 \\ \hline \end{array} \qquad \begin{array}{r} 1 \\ + 9 \\ \hline \end{array} \qquad \begin{array}{r} 2 \\ + 2 \\ \hline \end{array}$$

$$\begin{array}{r} 7 \\ + 7 \\ \hline \end{array} \qquad \begin{array}{r} 1 \\ + 3 \\ \hline \end{array} \qquad \begin{array}{r} 9 \\ + 9 \\ \hline \end{array} \qquad \begin{array}{r} 0 \\ + 3 \\ \hline \end{array} \qquad \begin{array}{r} 1 \\ + 1 \\ \hline \end{array}$$

$$\begin{array}{r} 0 \\ + 9 \\ \hline \end{array} \qquad \begin{array}{r} 4 \\ + 4 \\ \hline \end{array} \qquad \begin{array}{r} 1 \\ + 6 \\ \hline \end{array} \qquad \begin{array}{r} 4 \\ + 2 \\ \hline \end{array} \qquad \begin{array}{r} 6 \\ + 6 \\ \hline \end{array}$$

$$\begin{array}{r} 7 \\ + 1 \\ \hline \end{array} \qquad \begin{array}{r} 5 \\ + 5 \\ \hline \end{array} \qquad \begin{array}{r} 8 \\ + 0 \\ \hline \end{array} \qquad \begin{array}{r} 6 \\ + 6 \\ \hline \end{array} \qquad \begin{array}{r} 5 \\ + 1 \\ \hline \end{array}$$

$$\begin{array}{r} 8 \\ + 8 \\ \hline \end{array} \qquad \begin{array}{r} 2 \\ + 7 \\ \hline \end{array} \qquad \begin{array}{r} 3 \\ + 2 \\ \hline \end{array} \qquad \begin{array}{r} 8 \\ + 1 \\ \hline \end{array} \qquad \begin{array}{r} 2 \\ + 8 \\ \hline \end{array}$$

Score: _____

2-29Fb

Name _____

Date _____

Draw a picture and write a number sentence for this story. Write the answer with a label.

1. Tim had ten dimes. He gave three to his brother. How many dimes does Tim have now?

[ ]

Number sentence _____

Answer _____

2. Fill in the missing addends.

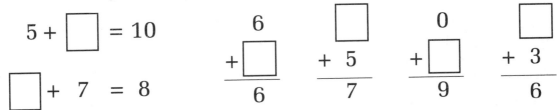

$$5 + \boxed{} = 10$$

$$\boxed{} + 7 = 8$$

$$\begin{array}{r} 6 \\ + \boxed{} \\ \hline 6 \end{array} \qquad \begin{array}{r} \boxed{} \\ + 5 \\ \hline 7 \end{array} \qquad \begin{array}{r} 0 \\ + \boxed{} \\ \hline 9 \end{array} \qquad \begin{array}{r} \boxed{} \\ + 3 \\ \hline 6 \end{array}$$

3. Use a crayon to circle all the even numbers in Problem 2.

4. Number the clock face.

    Show half past eleven.

5. How much money is this? _____

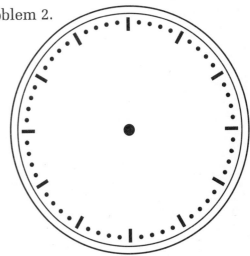

Name _____   **LESSON 29B**

Date _____   *Math 2*

Draw a picture and write a number sentence for this story. Write the answer with a label.

1. Angelo borrowed six books from the library. He read four books and took them back to the library. How many more books does he have left to read?

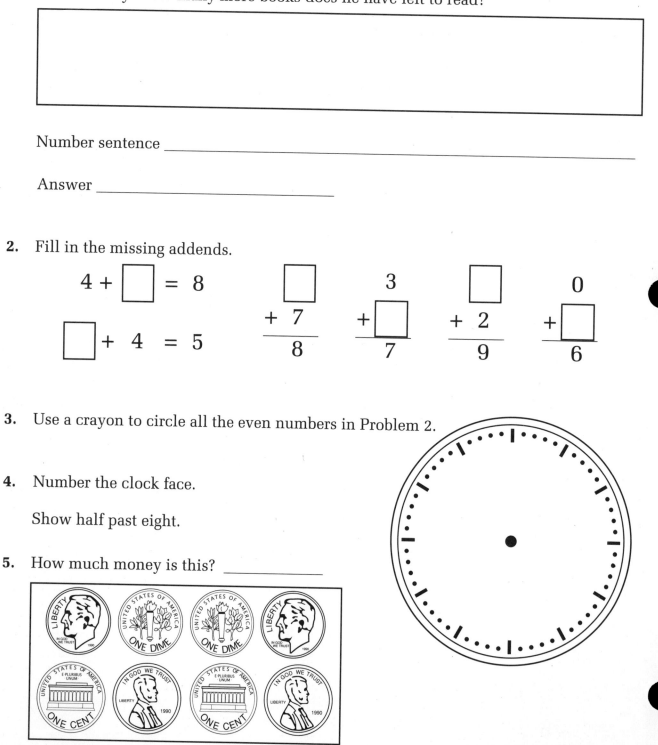

Number sentence _____

Answer _____

2. Fill in the missing addends.

$$4 + \boxed{} = 8$$

$$\boxed{} + 4 = 5$$

$$\begin{array}{r} \boxed{} \\ + 7 \\ \hline 8 \end{array} \qquad \begin{array}{r} 3 \\ + \boxed{} \\ \hline 7 \end{array} \qquad \begin{array}{r} \boxed{} \\ + 2 \\ \hline 9 \end{array} \qquad \begin{array}{r} 0 \\ + \boxed{} \\ \hline 6 \end{array}$$

3. Use a crayon to circle all the even numbers in Problem 2.

4. Number the clock face.

    Show half past eight.

5. How much money is this? _____

Name _____

Date _____

Draw a picture and write a number sentence for this story. Write the answer with a label.

1. Matthew wrote a five-page story. On the next day he added two pages to his story. How long is his story now?

    [ ]

    Number sentence _____

    Answer _____

2. Divide each shape in half. Shade one half of each shape.

3. Which number on the thermometer is the temperature closest to? _____ °F

4. Circle the largest number. | 17   34   29 |

5. Match each name with the correct piece.

    one half •

    one third •

    one sixth •

6. Add.

    7 + 2 = ____   3 + 2 = ____   2 + 6 = ____

    2 + 8 = ____   9 + 2 = ____   5 + 2 = ____

$$
\begin{array}{r} 3 \\ +\ 4 \\ \hline \end{array}
\qquad
\begin{array}{r} 6 \\ +\ 7 \\ \hline \end{array}
\qquad
\begin{array}{r} 9 \\ +\ 8 \\ \hline \end{array}
\qquad
\begin{array}{r} 5 \\ +\ 4 \\ \hline \end{array}
\qquad
\begin{array}{r} 7 \\ +\ 8 \\ \hline \end{array}
$$

$$
\begin{array}{r} 6 \\ +\ 5 \\ \hline \end{array}
\qquad
\begin{array}{r} 8 \\ +\ 9 \\ \hline \end{array}
\qquad
\begin{array}{r} 4 \\ +\ 3 \\ \hline \end{array}
\qquad
\begin{array}{r} 7 \\ +\ 6 \\ \hline \end{array}
\qquad
\begin{array}{r} 4 \\ +\ 5 \\ \hline \end{array}
$$

$$
\begin{array}{r} 8 \\ +\ 7 \\ \hline \end{array}
\qquad
\begin{array}{r} 3 \\ +\ 4 \\ \hline \end{array}
\qquad
\begin{array}{r} 5 \\ +\ 4 \\ \hline \end{array}
\qquad
\begin{array}{r} 9 \\ +\ 8 \\ \hline \end{array}
\qquad
\begin{array}{r} 5 \\ +\ 6 \\ \hline \end{array}
$$

$$
\begin{array}{r} 6 \\ +\ 7 \\ \hline \end{array}
\qquad
\begin{array}{r} 4 \\ +\ 5 \\ \hline \end{array}
\qquad
\begin{array}{r} 7 \\ +\ 8 \\ \hline \end{array}
\qquad
\begin{array}{r} 6 \\ +\ 5 \\ \hline \end{array}
\qquad
\begin{array}{r} 8 \\ +\ 9 \\ \hline \end{array}
$$

$$
\begin{array}{r} 3 \\ +\ 4 \\ \hline \end{array}
\qquad
\begin{array}{r} 7 \\ +\ 6 \\ \hline \end{array}
\qquad
\begin{array}{r} 5 \\ +\ 6 \\ \hline \end{array}
\qquad
\begin{array}{r} 9 \\ +\ 8 \\ \hline \end{array}
\qquad
\begin{array}{r} 8 \\ +\ 7 \\ \hline \end{array}
$$

Score: _____

$$
\begin{array}{r} 3 \\ +4 \\ \hline \end{array}
\qquad
\begin{array}{r} 6 \\ +7 \\ \hline \end{array}
\qquad
\begin{array}{r} 9 \\ +8 \\ \hline \end{array}
\qquad
\begin{array}{r} 5 \\ +4 \\ \hline \end{array}
\qquad
\begin{array}{r} 7 \\ +8 \\ \hline \end{array}
$$

$$
\begin{array}{r} 6 \\ +5 \\ \hline \end{array}
\qquad
\begin{array}{r} 8 \\ +9 \\ \hline \end{array}
\qquad
\begin{array}{r} 4 \\ +3 \\ \hline \end{array}
\qquad
\begin{array}{r} 7 \\ +6 \\ \hline \end{array}
\qquad
\begin{array}{r} 4 \\ +5 \\ \hline \end{array}
$$

$$
\begin{array}{r} 8 \\ +7 \\ \hline \end{array}
\qquad
\begin{array}{r} 3 \\ +4 \\ \hline \end{array}
\qquad
\begin{array}{r} 5 \\ +4 \\ \hline \end{array}
\qquad
\begin{array}{r} 9 \\ +8 \\ \hline \end{array}
\qquad
\begin{array}{r} 5 \\ +6 \\ \hline \end{array}
$$

$$
\begin{array}{r} 6 \\ +7 \\ \hline \end{array}
\qquad
\begin{array}{r} 4 \\ +5 \\ \hline \end{array}
\qquad
\begin{array}{r} 7 \\ +8 \\ \hline \end{array}
\qquad
\begin{array}{r} 6 \\ +5 \\ \hline \end{array}
\qquad
\begin{array}{r} 8 \\ +9 \\ \hline \end{array}
$$

$$
\begin{array}{r} 3 \\ +4 \\ \hline \end{array}
\qquad
\begin{array}{r} 7 \\ +6 \\ \hline \end{array}
\qquad
\begin{array}{r} 5 \\ +6 \\ \hline \end{array}
\qquad
\begin{array}{r} 9 \\ +8 \\ \hline \end{array}
\qquad
\begin{array}{r} 8 \\ +7 \\ \hline \end{array}
$$

Score: _____

2-31Fa

Name _____

Date _____

Draw a picture and write a number sentence for this story. Write the answer with a label.

1. Shawn has 2 dimes and 5 pennies. Steven has 3 dimes and 4 pennies. How many dimes do the two boys have together?

    [ ]

    Number sentence _____

    Answer _____

2. Draw tally marks to show **13**.

    [ ]

3. How much money is this? _____

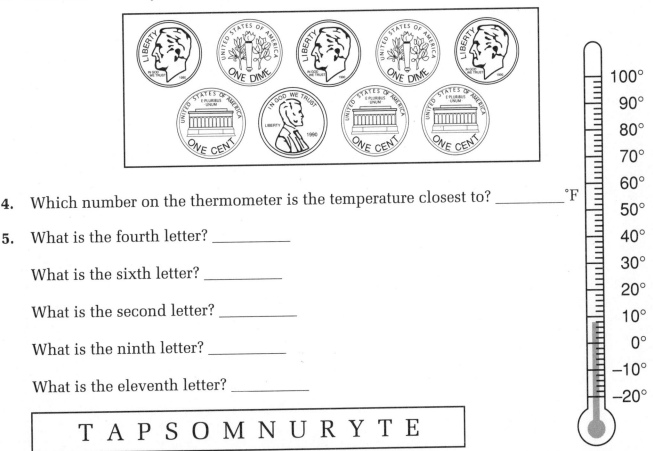

4. Which number on the thermometer is the temperature closest to? _____°F

5. What is the fourth letter? _____

    What is the sixth letter? _____

    What is the second letter? _____

    What is the ninth letter? _____

    What is the eleventh letter? _____

    | T A P S O M N U R Y T E |

Name _____

Date _____

Draw a picture and write a number sentence for this story. Write the answer with a label.

1. Shawn has 2 dimes and 5 pennies. Steven has 3 dimes and 4 pennies. How many pennies do the two boys have together?

    Number sentence _____

    Answer _____

2. Draw tally marks to show **17**.

3. How much money is this? _____

4. Which number on the thermometer is the temperature closest to? _____ °F

5. What is the sixth letter? _____

    What is the fifth letter? _____

    What is the seventh letter? _____

    What is the twelfth letter? _____

    What is the tenth letter? _____

    T A P S O M N U R Y T E

Cut along the dotted lines.

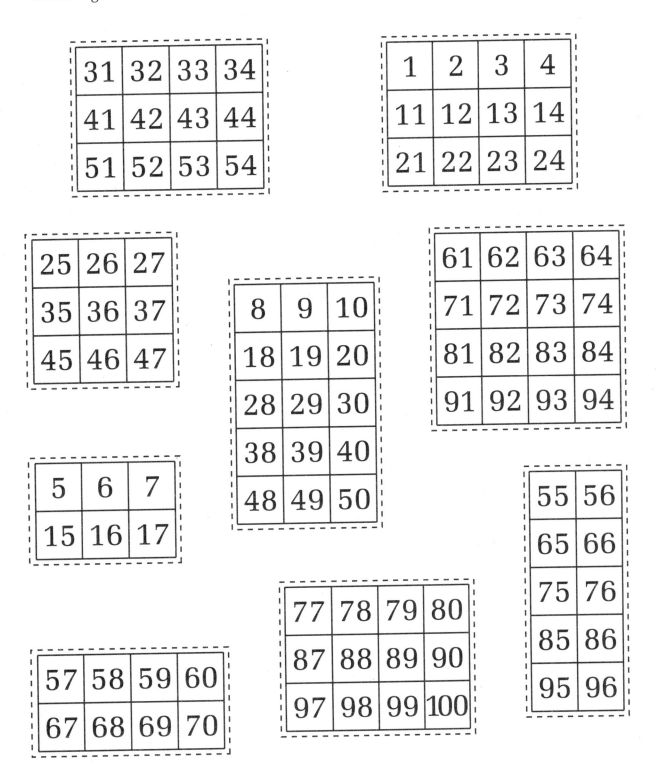

2 + 0	2 + 6	3 + 3	1 + 9	2 + 2
7 + 7	1 + 3	9 + 9	0 + 3	1 + 1
0 + 9	4 + 4	1 + 6	4 + 2	6 + 6
7 + 1	5 + 5	8 + 0	6 + 6	5 + 1
8 + 8	2 + 7	3 + 2	8 + 1	2 + 8

Score: _____

2-32Fa

Name _____ **LESSON 32A**

Math 2

Date _____

Draw a picture and write a number sentence for this story. Write the answer with a label.

1. Scott had 12 balloons. Two popped. How many balloons does he have now?

   [box]

   Number sentence _____

   Answer _____

2. Trace the horizontal line segment with a red crayon.

   Trace the vertical line segment with a blue crayon.

   Trace the oblique line segment with a yellow crayon.

   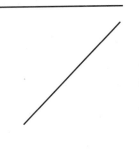

3. Divide each shape in half. Shade one half.

   [rectangle] [triangle] [square]

4. Use the "Weekday Wake-up Times" graph to answer these questions.

   How many children wake up at half past seven? _____

   At what time do the most children wake up? _____

5. How many tally marks are shown? _____

   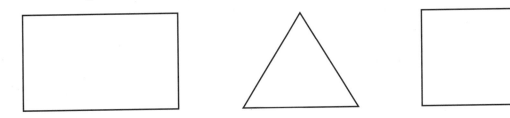

2-32Wa

Name _____

Date _____

Draw a picture and write a number sentence for this story. Write the answer with a label.

1. Nicole had seven markers. She gave two markers to her friend Jessica. How many markers does Nicole have now?

    +--+
    | |
    | |
    | |
    | |
    +--+

    Number sentence _____

    Answer _____

2. Trace the horizontal line segment with a red crayon.

    Trace the vertical line segment with a blue crayon.

    Trace the oblique line segment with a yellow crayon.

3. Divide each shape in half. Shade one half.

    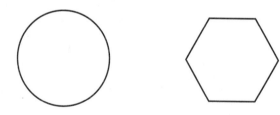

4. Number the clock face. Show half past four on the clock.

    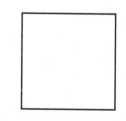

5. How many tally marks are shown? _____

    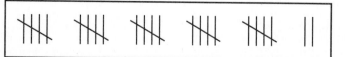

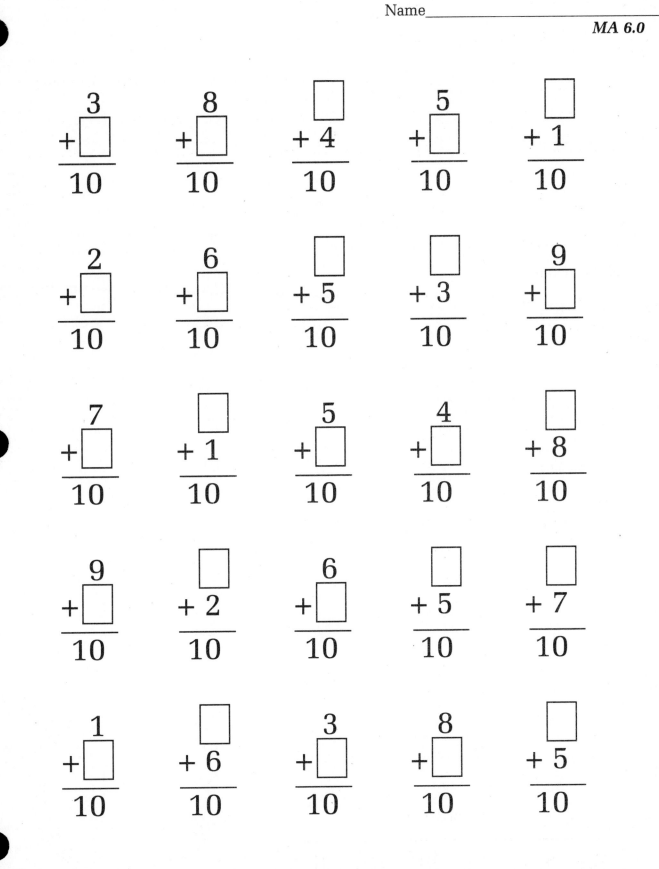

$$\begin{array}{r} 3 \\ +\ \square \\ \hline 10 \end{array} \qquad \begin{array}{r} 8 \\ +\ \square \\ \hline 10 \end{array} \qquad \begin{array}{r} \square \\ +\ 4 \\ \hline 10 \end{array} \qquad \begin{array}{r} 5 \\ +\ \square \\ \hline 10 \end{array} \qquad \begin{array}{r} \square \\ +\ 1 \\ \hline 10 \end{array}$$

$$\begin{array}{r} 2 \\ +\ \square \\ \hline 10 \end{array} \qquad \begin{array}{r} 6 \\ +\ \square \\ \hline 10 \end{array} \qquad \begin{array}{r} \square \\ +\ 5 \\ \hline 10 \end{array} \qquad \begin{array}{r} \square \\ +\ 3 \\ \hline 10 \end{array} \qquad \begin{array}{r} 9 \\ +\ \square \\ \hline 10 \end{array}$$

$$\begin{array}{r} 7 \\ +\ \square \\ \hline 10 \end{array} \qquad \begin{array}{r} \square \\ +\ 1 \\ \hline 10 \end{array} \qquad \begin{array}{r} 5 \\ +\ \square \\ \hline 10 \end{array} \qquad \begin{array}{r} 4 \\ +\ \square \\ \hline 10 \end{array} \qquad \begin{array}{r} \square \\ +\ 8 \\ \hline 10 \end{array}$$

$$\begin{array}{r} 9 \\ +\ \square \\ \hline 10 \end{array} \qquad \begin{array}{r} \square \\ +\ 2 \\ \hline 10 \end{array} \qquad \begin{array}{r} 6 \\ +\ \square \\ \hline 10 \end{array} \qquad \begin{array}{r} \square \\ +\ 5 \\ \hline 10 \end{array} \qquad \begin{array}{r} \square \\ +\ 7 \\ \hline 10 \end{array}$$

$$\begin{array}{r} 1 \\ +\ \square \\ \hline 10 \end{array} \qquad \begin{array}{r} \square \\ +\ 6 \\ \hline 10 \end{array} \qquad \begin{array}{r} 3 \\ +\ \square \\ \hline 10 \end{array} \qquad \begin{array}{r} 8 \\ +\ \square \\ \hline 10 \end{array} \qquad \begin{array}{r} \square \\ +\ 5 \\ \hline 10 \end{array}$$

Score:_____

Name _____

LESSON 33A

Math 2

Date _____

Draw a picture and write a number sentence for this story. Write the answer with a label.

1. Six children got on Bus A at the first stop. Five more children got on Bus A at the second stop. How many children are on Bus A now?

    ┌───┐
    │   │
    │   │
    │   │
    │   │
    └───┘

    Number sentence _____

    Answer _____

2. Use a red crayon to trace the horizontal line segments in these letters.
    Use a blue crayon to trace the vertical line segments in these letters.
    Use a yellow crayon to trace the oblique line segments in these letters.

3. Draw a tally mark for each letter of the alphabet.

    ┌───┐
    │   │
    │   │
    └───┘

    How many tally marks did you draw? _____

4. Fill in the missing addends for the sums of 10.

    ☐ + 2 = 10   1 + ☐ = 10   ☐ + 4 = 10

    ☐ + 7 = 10   5 + ☐ = 10   0 + ☐ = 10

5. How much money is 6 dimes? _____

    How much money is 54 pennies? _____

    Circle the one that is worth the most.

Name _____   **LESSON 33B**
                                         Math 2
Date _____

Draw a picture and write a number sentence for this story. Write the answer with a label.

1. Seven children got on Bus B at the first stop. Six more children got on Bus B at the second stop. How many children are on Bus B now?

    ┌───┐
    │   │
    │   │
    │   │
    │   │
    │   │
    └───┘

    Number sentence _____

    Answer _____

2. Use a red crayon to trace the horizontal line segments in these letters.
    Use a blue crayon to trace the vertical line segments in these letters.
    Use a yellow crayon to trace the oblique line segments in these letters.

3. Ask someone in your family to let you tally the number of coins in their pocket or wallet. Draw one tally mark for each coin.

    ┌───┐
    │   │
    │   │
    └───┘

    How many coins is this? _____

4. Fill in the missing addends for the sums of 10.

    $\boxed{} + 2 = 10$ $1 + \boxed{} = 10$ $\boxed{} + 4 = 10$

    $\boxed{} + 7 = 10$ $5 + \boxed{} = 10$ $0 + \boxed{} = 10$

5. How much money is 7 dimes? _____

    How much money is 39 pennies? _____

    Circle the one that is worth the most.

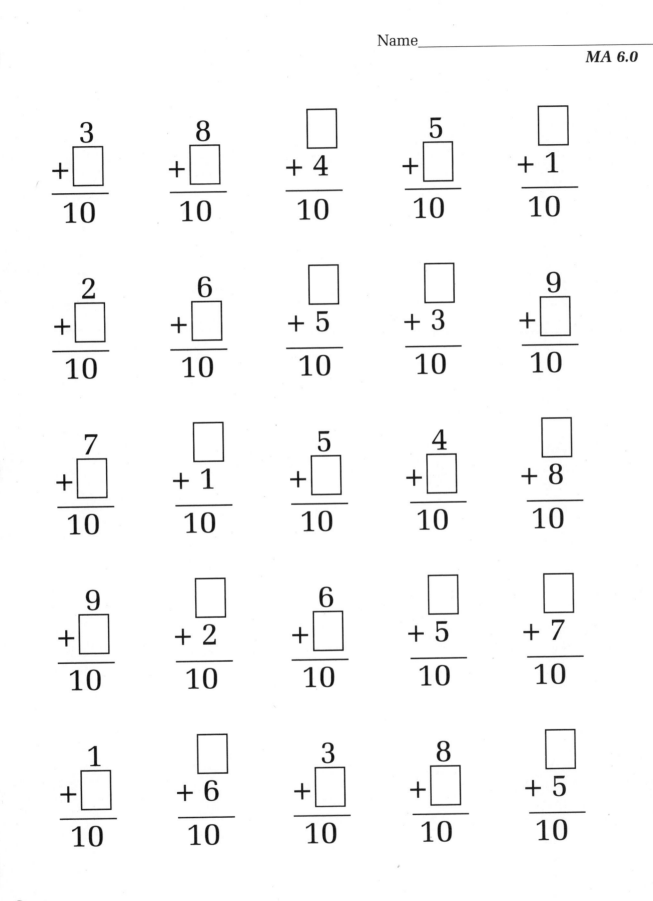

$$
\begin{array}{r} 3 \\ +\ \square \\ \hline 10 \end{array}
\qquad
\begin{array}{r} 8 \\ +\ \square \\ \hline 10 \end{array}
\qquad
\begin{array}{r} \square \\ +\ 4 \\ \hline 10 \end{array}
\qquad
\begin{array}{r} 5 \\ +\ \square \\ \hline 10 \end{array}
\qquad
\begin{array}{r} \square \\ +\ 1 \\ \hline 10 \end{array}
$$

$$
\begin{array}{r} 2 \\ +\ \square \\ \hline 10 \end{array}
\qquad
\begin{array}{r} 6 \\ +\ \square \\ \hline 10 \end{array}
\qquad
\begin{array}{r} \square \\ +\ 5 \\ \hline 10 \end{array}
\qquad
\begin{array}{r} \square \\ +\ 3 \\ \hline 10 \end{array}
\qquad
\begin{array}{r} 9 \\ +\ \square \\ \hline 10 \end{array}
$$

$$
\begin{array}{r} 7 \\ +\ \square \\ \hline 10 \end{array}
\qquad
\begin{array}{r} \square \\ +\ 1 \\ \hline 10 \end{array}
\qquad
\begin{array}{r} 5 \\ +\ \square \\ \hline 10 \end{array}
\qquad
\begin{array}{r} 4 \\ +\ \square \\ \hline 10 \end{array}
\qquad
\begin{array}{r} \square \\ +\ 8 \\ \hline 10 \end{array}
$$

$$
\begin{array}{r} 9 \\ +\ \square \\ \hline 10 \end{array}
\qquad
\begin{array}{r} \square \\ +\ 2 \\ \hline 10 \end{array}
\qquad
\begin{array}{r} 6 \\ +\ \square \\ \hline 10 \end{array}
\qquad
\begin{array}{r} \square \\ +\ 5 \\ \hline 10 \end{array}
\qquad
\begin{array}{r} \square \\ +\ 7 \\ \hline 10 \end{array}
$$

$$
\begin{array}{r} 1 \\ +\ \square \\ \hline 10 \end{array}
\qquad
\begin{array}{r} \square \\ +\ 6 \\ \hline 10 \end{array}
\qquad
\begin{array}{r} 3 \\ +\ \square \\ \hline 10 \end{array}
\qquad
\begin{array}{r} 8 \\ +\ \square \\ \hline 10 \end{array}
\qquad
\begin{array}{r} \square \\ +\ 5 \\ \hline 10 \end{array}
$$

Score:_____

2-34Fa

Name _____

Date _____

1. Each weekday Paul eats a bowl of cereal for breakfast. How many bowls of cereal will Paul eat in one week? _____

2. Draw tally marks to show the number of children in this classroom.

   [ ]

   How many tally marks is this? _____

3. Divide the circle in half.   Divide the circle into fourths.

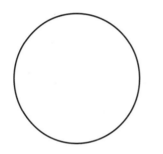   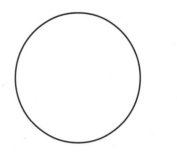

4. It's half past five now.
   What time was it one hour ago?
   Show this time on both clocks.

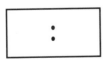

5. Use a red crayon to circle the even numbers on the clock face.

6. How much money is 2 dimes? _____

   How much money is 30 pennies? _____

   Circle the one that is worth the most.

2-34Wa

1. Each weekday Debbie eats a muffin for breakfast. How many muffins will Debbie eat in one week? _____

2. Draw tally marks to show the number of people in your family.

    How many tally marks is this? _____

3. Color the whole circle yellow.
   Color the circle divided into halves blue.
   Color the circle divided into fourths red.
   Color the circle divided into eighths green.

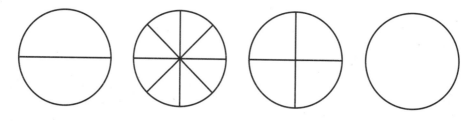

4. It's half past three now.
   What time was it one hour ago?
   Show this time on both clocks.

5. Circle the odd numbers on the clock face.

6. How much money is 6 dimes? _____

   How much money is 42 pennies? _____

   Circle the one that is worth the most.

Name _____

Date _____

Draw a picture and write a number sentence for this story. Write the answer with a label.

1. Kathy had eight pencils. Her sister gave her two more. How many pencils does Kathy have now?

    +--+
    | |
    | |
    | |
    | |
    +--+

    Number sentence _____

    Answer _____

2. Show two different ways to divide a square in half. Color one half of each square.

    □   □

3. How much money is this? _____

4. What is the second day of the week? _____

    What is the fifth month of the year? _____

    What is the last month of the year? _____

    What is the sixth day of the week? _____

5. Circle the odd numbers.   4   9   6   3   11   8   12   7

6. Find the sums.

    0 + 4 = _____   4 + 2 = _____   2 + 9 = _____   8 + 8 = _____

    6 + 6 = _____   8 + 1 = _____   1 + 5 = _____   6 + 2 = _____

$$\begin{array}{r} 3 \\ + 4 \\ \hline \end{array} \qquad \begin{array}{r} 6 \\ + 7 \\ \hline \end{array} \qquad \begin{array}{r} 9 \\ + 8 \\ \hline \end{array} \qquad \begin{array}{r} 5 \\ + 4 \\ \hline \end{array} \qquad \begin{array}{r} 7 \\ + 8 \\ \hline \end{array}$$

$$\begin{array}{r} 6 \\ + 5 \\ \hline \end{array} \qquad \begin{array}{r} 8 \\ + 9 \\ \hline \end{array} \qquad \begin{array}{r} 4 \\ + 3 \\ \hline \end{array} \qquad \begin{array}{r} 7 \\ + 6 \\ \hline \end{array} \qquad \begin{array}{r} 4 \\ + 5 \\ \hline \end{array}$$

$$\begin{array}{r} 8 \\ + 7 \\ \hline \end{array} \qquad \begin{array}{r} 3 \\ + 4 \\ \hline \end{array} \qquad \begin{array}{r} 5 \\ + 4 \\ \hline \end{array} \qquad \begin{array}{r} 9 \\ + 8 \\ \hline \end{array} \qquad \begin{array}{r} 5 \\ + 6 \\ \hline \end{array}$$

$$\begin{array}{r} 6 \\ + 7 \\ \hline \end{array} \qquad \begin{array}{r} 4 \\ + 5 \\ \hline \end{array} \qquad \begin{array}{r} 7 \\ + 8 \\ \hline \end{array} \qquad \begin{array}{r} 6 \\ + 5 \\ \hline \end{array} \qquad \begin{array}{r} 8 \\ + 9 \\ \hline \end{array}$$

$$\begin{array}{r} 3 \\ + 4 \\ \hline \end{array} \qquad \begin{array}{r} 7 \\ + 6 \\ \hline \end{array} \qquad \begin{array}{r} 5 \\ + 6 \\ \hline \end{array} \qquad \begin{array}{r} 9 \\ + 8 \\ \hline \end{array} \qquad \begin{array}{r} 8 \\ + 7 \\ \hline \end{array}$$

Score: _____

Name _____

Date _____

1. What is the fifth day of the week? _____

   What day of the week was yesterday? _____

   What is the eleventh month of the year? _____

2. Use the classroom graphs to answer these questions.

   How many children wake up at 6:30? _____

   How many children have a birthday in July or August? _____

3. Fill in the missing numbers on this piece of a hundred number chart.

61			64
71			
81		83	
91			94

4. Draw a horizontal line.   Draw a vertical line.   Draw an oblique line.

5. Find each sum.

   60 + 10 = _____   40 + 10 = _____   10 + 80 = _____

6. Write three addition facts that have sums that are even numbers.

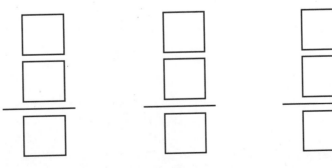

Name _____ **LESSON 35B**

Date _____ *Math 2*

1. What is the second day of the week? _____

   What day of the week will it be tomorrow? _____

   What is the tenth month of the year? _____

2. Draw a horizontal line.   Draw a vertical line.   Draw an oblique line.

3. Fill in the missing numbers on this piece of a hundred number chart.

77			
87		89	
97			100

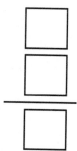

100°
90°
80°
70°
60°
50°
40°
30°
20°
10°
0°
−10°
−20°

4. Which number on the
   thermometer is the temperature closest to? _____°F

5. Find each sum.

   30 + 10 = _____   10 + 70 = _____   20 + 10 = _____

6. Write three addition facts that have sums that are odd numbers.

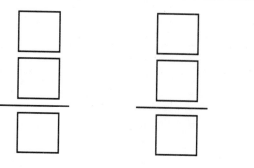

-35Wb

3 + 4	6 + 7	9 + 8	5 + 4	7 + 8
6 + 5	8 + 9	4 + 3	7 + 6	4 + 5
8 + 7	3 + 4	5 + 4	9 + 8	5 + 6
6 + 7	4 + 5	7 + 8	6 + 5	8 + 9
3 + 4	7 + 6	5 + 6	9 + 8	8 + 7

Score: _____

2-36Fa

Name _____   **LESSON 36A**

Date _____   *Math 2*

Draw a picture and write a number sentence for this story. Write the answer with a label.

1. Judith had 20 hair ribbons. Her aunt gave her 10 more. How many hair ribbons does she have now?

   [box]

   Number sentence _____

   Answer _____

2. How many socks are in the box? _____

   Circle pairs of socks.

   How many pairs of socks are there? _____

   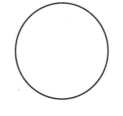

3. Fill in the missing numbers on this piece of a hundred number chart.

23			26		
		35			
43					48

4. Divide the circle into fourths.

5. Find the sums.   20 + 10 = _____   70 + 10 = _____

6. Fill in the missing addends.   ☐ + 2 = 10   6 + ☐ = 10

Name _____   **LESSON 36B**

Date _____   *Math 2*

Draw a picture and write a number sentence for this story. Write the answer with a label.

1. Rebecca's dog ate 30 dog biscuits last week. This week he ate 10 biscuits. How many dog biscuits did he eat altogether?

    ┌───┐
    │   │
    │   │
    │   │
    └───┘

    Number sentence _____

    Answer _____

2. How many socks are in the box? _____

    Circle pairs of socks.

    How many pairs of socks are there? _____

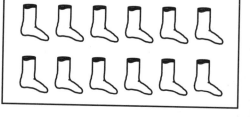

3. Fill in the missing numbers on this piece of a hundred number chart.

42			
			55
62			
		74	

4. Divide these shapes in half.

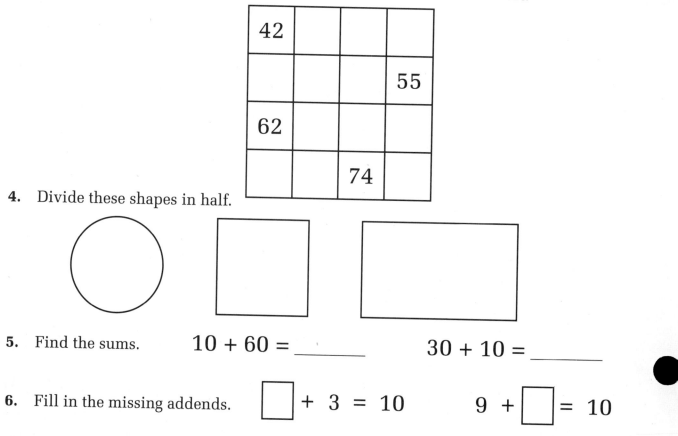

5. Find the sums.   10 + 60 = _____   30 + 10 = _____

6. Fill in the missing addends.   ☐ + 3 = 10   9 + ☐ = 10

2-36Wb

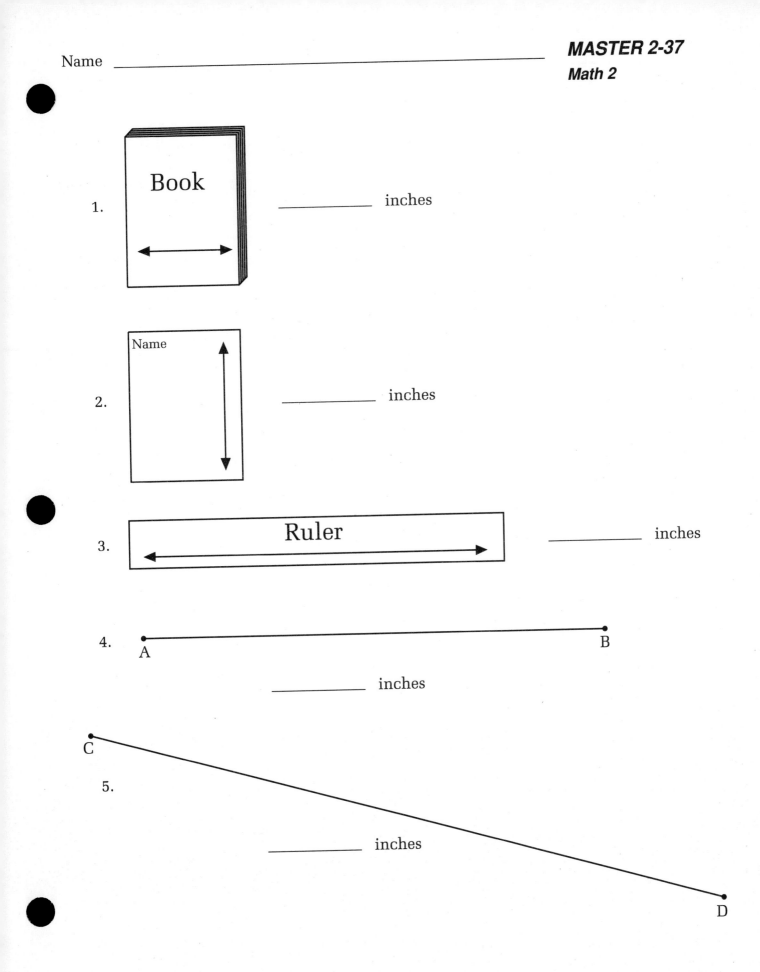

1. Book _____ inches

2. Name _____ inches

3. Ruler _____ inches

4. A ———— B
_____ inches

5. C
_____ inches
D

$$
\begin{array}{r} 6 \\ +\,5 \\ \hline \end{array}
\qquad
\begin{array}{r} 7 \\ +\,1 \\ \hline \end{array}
\qquad
\begin{array}{r} 9 \\ +\,8 \\ \hline \end{array}
\qquad
\begin{array}{r} 7 \\ +\,7 \\ \hline \end{array}
\qquad
\begin{array}{r} 3 \\ +\,4 \\ \hline \end{array}
$$

$$
\begin{array}{r} 7 \\ +\,8 \\ \hline \end{array}
\qquad
\begin{array}{r} 0 \\ +\,8 \\ \hline \end{array}
\qquad
\begin{array}{r} 9 \\ +\,1 \\ \hline \end{array}
\qquad
\begin{array}{r} 3 \\ +\,4 \\ \hline \end{array}
\qquad
\begin{array}{r} 4 \\ +\,5 \\ \hline \end{array}
$$

$$
\begin{array}{r} 5 \\ +\,5 \\ \hline \end{array}
\qquad
\begin{array}{r} 4 \\ +\,2 \\ \hline \end{array}
\qquad
\begin{array}{r} 6 \\ +\,7 \\ \hline \end{array}
\qquad
\begin{array}{r} 7 \\ +\,2 \\ \hline \end{array}
\qquad
\begin{array}{r} 8 \\ +\,8 \\ \hline \end{array}
$$

$$
\begin{array}{r} 8 \\ +\,7 \\ \hline \end{array}
\qquad
\begin{array}{r} 5 \\ +\,4 \\ \hline \end{array}
\qquad
\begin{array}{r} 1 \\ +\,8 \\ \hline \end{array}
\qquad
\begin{array}{r} 2 \\ +\,8 \\ \hline \end{array}
\qquad
\begin{array}{r} 8 \\ +\,9 \\ \hline \end{array}
$$

$$
\begin{array}{r} 2 \\ +\,6 \\ \hline \end{array}
\qquad
\begin{array}{r} 3 \\ +\,2 \\ \hline \end{array}
\qquad
\begin{array}{r} 9 \\ +\,9 \\ \hline \end{array}
\qquad
\begin{array}{r} 6 \\ +\,7 \\ \hline \end{array}
\qquad
\begin{array}{r} 7 \\ +\,7 \\ \hline \end{array}
$$

Score: _____

Name _____

Date _____

Draw a picture and write a number sentence for this story. Write the answer with a label.

1. Leroy ate a peanut butter sandwich every day last week. This week he ate two peanut butter sandwiches. How many peanut butter sandwiches did he eat?

[ ]

Number sentence _____

Answer _____

2. How many shoes are in the box? _____

Circle pairs of shoes.

How many pairs of shoes are there? _____

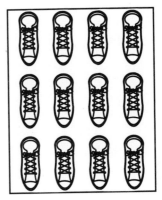

3. How many tally marks are shown? _____

| HHL   HHL   HHL   HHL   I |

4. Write the names of the first six months.

1. _____   2. _____   3. _____

4. _____   5. _____   6. _____

5. Color the even numbers red. Color the odd numbers yellow.

1	2	3	4	5	6	7	8	9	10
11	12	13	14	15	16	17	18	19	20

Name _____   **LESSON 37B**
                                            Math 2
Date _____

Draw a picture and write a number sentence for this story. Write the answer with a label.

1. There were 9 pickles in the jar. Lynn ate three pickles. How many pickles are left?

```
┌──────────────────────────────────────────────────────┐
│                                                        │
│                                                        │
│                                                        │
│                                                        │
└──────────────────────────────────────────────────────┘
```

Number sentence _____

Answer _____

2. How many shoes are in the box? _____

Circle pairs of shoes.

How many pairs of shoes are there? _____

3. How many tally marks are shown? _____

```
┌──────────────────────────────────────────────┐
│         |||| |   |||| |   |||| |   ||||        │
└──────────────────────────────────────────────┘
```

4. Fill in the missing months.

_____ ,   March,   _____

5. Color the answers to these examples.

$$1 + 1 = \qquad 2 + 2 = \qquad 3 + 3 = \qquad 4 + 4 = \qquad 5 + 5 =$$
$$6 + 6 = \qquad 7 + 7 = \qquad 8 + 8 = \qquad 9 + 9 = \qquad 10 + 10 =$$

1	2	3	4	5	6	7	8	9	10
11	12	13	14	15	16	17	18	19	20

2-37Wb

$$\begin{array}{r} 3 \\ +\ \square \\ \hline 10 \end{array} \qquad \begin{array}{r} 8 \\ +\ \square \\ \hline 10 \end{array} \qquad \begin{array}{r} \square \\ +\ 4 \\ \hline 10 \end{array} \qquad \begin{array}{r} 5 \\ +\ \square \\ \hline 10 \end{array} \qquad \begin{array}{r} \square \\ +\ 1 \\ \hline 10 \end{array}$$

$$\begin{array}{r} 2 \\ +\ \square \\ \hline 10 \end{array} \qquad \begin{array}{r} 6 \\ +\ \square \\ \hline 10 \end{array} \qquad \begin{array}{r} \square \\ +\ 5 \\ \hline 10 \end{array} \qquad \begin{array}{r} \square \\ +\ 3 \\ \hline 10 \end{array} \qquad \begin{array}{r} 9 \\ +\ \square \\ \hline 10 \end{array}$$

$$\begin{array}{r} 7 \\ +\ \square \\ \hline 10 \end{array} \qquad \begin{array}{r} \square \\ +\ 1 \\ \hline 10 \end{array} \qquad \begin{array}{r} 5 \\ +\ \square \\ \hline 10 \end{array} \qquad \begin{array}{r} 4 \\ +\ \square \\ \hline 10 \end{array} \qquad \begin{array}{r} \square \\ +\ 8 \\ \hline 10 \end{array}$$

$$\begin{array}{r} 9 \\ +\ \square \\ \hline 10 \end{array} \qquad \begin{array}{r} \square \\ +\ 2 \\ \hline 10 \end{array} \qquad \begin{array}{r} 6 \\ +\ \square \\ \hline 10 \end{array} \qquad \begin{array}{r} \square \\ +\ 5 \\ \hline 10 \end{array} \qquad \begin{array}{r} \square \\ +\ 7 \\ \hline 10 \end{array}$$

$$\begin{array}{r} 1 \\ +\ \square \\ \hline 10 \end{array} \qquad \begin{array}{r} \square \\ +\ 6 \\ \hline 10 \end{array} \qquad \begin{array}{r} 3 \\ +\ \square \\ \hline 10 \end{array} \qquad \begin{array}{r} 8 \\ +\ \square \\ \hline 10 \end{array} \qquad \begin{array}{r} \square \\ +\ 5 \\ \hline 10 \end{array}$$

Score:_____

2-38Fa

Date _____

Draw a picture and write a number sentence for this story. Write the answer with a label.

1. Tom has 3 red markers, 4 green markers, and 2 pencils. How many markers does Tom have?

    ```
    ┌──────────────────────────────────────────────────────┐
    │                                                      │
    │                                                      │
    │                                                      │
    └──────────────────────────────────────────────────────┘
    ```

    Number sentence _____

    Answer _____

2. How many tens and ones are in 49? _____ tens _____ ones

3. Write the names of the days of the week.

    1. _____ 2. _____ 3. _____ 4. _____

    5. _____ 6. _____ 7. _____

4. Circle all the squares that are divided into fourths (four equal parts).

5. Number the clock face. Show half past twelve on the clock face.

6. Circle the odd numbers on the clock face.

Name _____

Date _____

Draw a picture and write a number sentence for this story. Write the answer with a label.

1. Ken's mom gave him 4 chocolate chip cookies, 1 apple, 2 peanut butter cookies, and a drink box for the field trip. How many cookies did she give him?

    ┌───┐
    │   │
    │   │
    │   │
    └───┘

    Number sentence _____

    Answer _____

2. How many tens and ones are in 68?   _____ tens   _____ ones

3. What is the second day of the week? _____

    What is the fourth day of the week? _____

    What is the first day of the week? _____

    What is the sixth day of the week? _____

4. Underline all the circles that are divided into fourths (four equal parts).

5. Number the clock face. Show half past ten on the clock face.

6. Circle the even numbers on the clock face.

Name _____

6 + 5	7 + 1	9 + 8	7 + 7	3 + 4
7 + 8	0 + 8	9 + 1	3 + 4	4 + 5
5 + 5	4 + 2	6 + 7	7 + 2	8 + 8
8 + 7	5 + 4	1 + 8	2 + 8	8 + 9
2 + 6	3 + 2	9 + 9	6 + 7	7 + 7

Score: _____

2-39Fa

Name _____   **LESSON 39A**

Math 2

Date _____

Draw a picture and write a number sentence for this story. Write the answer with a label.

1. Corrine has 5 dogs, 2 cats, 3 birds, and a turtle as pets. How many of her pets have fur?

    Number sentence _____

    Answer _____

2. Finish the patterns.

    2, 4, 6, ___ , ___ , ___ , ___ , ___ , ___ , ___

    5, 10, 15, ___ , ___ , ___ , ___ , ___ , ___ , ___

3. Draw tally marks for **23**.

4. Write the names of the last 6 months of the year.

    7. _____   8. _____   9. _____

    10. _____   11. _____   12. _____

5. Make 82¢ using the fewest number of dimes and pennies. _____ dimes _____ pennies

    Make 37 using the fewest number of tens and ones. _____ tens _____ ones

6. Fill in the missing addends.

$$\begin{array}{r} 6 \\ +\ \square \\ \hline 10 \end{array} \qquad \begin{array}{r} \square \\ +\ 2 \\ \hline 7 \end{array} \qquad \begin{array}{r} 1 \\ +\ \square \\ \hline 6 \end{array} \qquad \begin{array}{r} \square \\ +\ 3 \\ \hline 7 \end{array}$$

$$7 + \square = 10$$

$$\square + 2 = 8$$

Name _____

Date _____

Math 2

Draw a picture and write a number sentence for this story. Write the answer with a label.

1. Chris has a collection of 3 helicopters, 1 fire engine, 2 police cars, 1 motorcycle, and 2 airplanes. If the toys were real, how many of them could fly?

    Number sentence _____

    Answer _____

2. Finish the patterns.

    1, 3, 5, ___ , ___ , ___ , ___ , ___ , ___ , ___

    10, 20, 30, ___ , ___ , ___ , ___ , ___ , ___ , ___

3. Draw tally marks for **17**.

5. What is the month before November? _____

    What is the month after July? _____

    What is the month before September? _____

5. Make 57¢ using the fewest number of dimes and pennies. _____ dimes _____ pennies

    Make 29 using the fewest number of tens and ones. _____ tens _____ ones

6. Fill in the missing addends.

$$\begin{array}{r} 2 \\ +\square \\ \hline 10 \end{array} \qquad \begin{array}{r} \square \\ +\ 1 \\ \hline 9 \end{array} \qquad \begin{array}{r} 4 \\ +\square \\ \hline 8 \end{array} \qquad \begin{array}{r} \square \\ +\ 7 \\ \hline 13 \end{array} \qquad \begin{array}{l} 3 + \square = 10 \\ \\ \square + 2 = 6 \end{array}$$

Name _____

Date _____

Draw a picture and write a number sentence for this story. Write the answer with a label.

1. Simone helped her brother bake cupcakes. There were 12 cupcakes. They gave five cupcakes to their neighbors. How many cupcakes do they have left?

    ┌───┐
    │   │
    │   │
    │   │
    └───┘

    Number sentence _____

    Answer _____

2. Show 32 using tally marks.

3. How much money is this? _____

4. Number the clock face. Show half past eight on both clocks.

    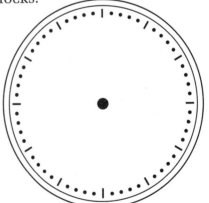

5. Use "The Weekday Wake-up Time" class graph to answer these questions.

    How many children wake up at 7:00? _____

    At what time do most children wake up? _____

    What is the latest time that someone in this class wakes up? _____

6. Find the sums.

    $4 + 5 =$ _____ $7 + 6 =$ _____ $8 + 9 =$ _____ $3 + 4 =$ _____

6	7	9	7	3
+ 5	+ 1	+ 8	+ 7	+ 4

7	0	9	3	4
+ 8	+ 8	+ 1	+ 4	+ 5

5	4	6	7	8
+ 5	+ 2	+ 7	+ 2	+ 8

8	5	1	2	8
+ 7	+ 4	+ 8	+ 8	+ 9

2	3	9	6	7
+ 6	+ 2	+ 9	+ 7	+ 7

Score: _____

2-40Fa

4 + 3	4 + 5	2 + 8	6 + 6	6 + 5
7 + 6	3 + 7	5 + 4	2 + 7	5 + 1
4 + 6	3 + 4	1 + 9	8 + 2	5 + 5
3 + 3	6 + 2	8 + 9	7 + 3	2 + 0
3 + 7	0 + 5	4 + 4	7 + 8	1 + 8

Score: _____

Name _____   **LESSON 41A**
                                                    Math 2
Date _____

Draw a picture and write a number sentence for the story. Write the answer with a label.

1. Stephanie and four of her friends were playing outside. Three more friends came to play. How many children are playing now?

    ┌───┐
    │   │
    │   │
    │   │
    │   │
    └───┘

    Number sentence _____

    Answer _____

2. Circle pairs of socks.

    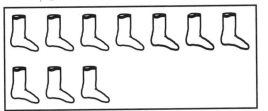   How many socks are in the box? _____

                                  How many pairs of socks are there? _____

                                  Count by 5's to find the number
                                  of toes in all of the socks.   _____ toes

3. Shade two fourths.   Shade four eighths.   Shade one half.

4. Make **73¢** using the fewest number of dimes and pennies.   ____ dimes ____ pennies.

    Make **16** using the fewest number of tens and ones.   ____ tens ____ ones

5. Add.

    $60 + 10 =$ ____ $30 + 10 =$ ____ $10 + 80 =$ ____

Name _____   **LESSON 41B**

Date _____   *Math 2*

Draw a picture and write a number sentence for the story. Write the answer with a label.

1. Colin and three of his friends were making a puzzle. Colin's two sisters came to help. How many children are working on the puzzle now?

   _____

   Number sentence _____

   Answer _____

2. Circle pairs of shoes.

   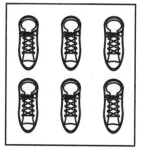

   How many shoes are in the box? _____

   How many pairs of shoes are there? _____

   Count by 5's to find the number
   of toes in all of the shoes.   _____ toes

3. Shade three fourths.   Shade three eighths.   Shade one half.

   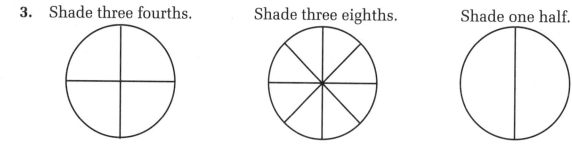

4. Make **27¢** using the fewest number of dimes and pennies.   ____ dimes ____ pennies.

   Make **45** using the fewest number of tens and ones.   ____ tens ____ ones

5. Add.

   $70 + 10 =$ ____ $20 + 10 =$ ____ $10 + 90 =$ ____

$$\begin{array}{r} 1 \\ + 9 \\ \hline \end{array} \qquad \begin{array}{r} 9 \\ + 8 \\ \hline \end{array} \qquad \begin{array}{r} 9 \\ + 7 \\ \hline \end{array} \qquad \begin{array}{r} 9 \\ + 9 \\ \hline \end{array} \qquad \begin{array}{r} 9 \\ + 2 \\ \hline \end{array}$$

$$\begin{array}{r} 9 \\ + 3 \\ \hline \end{array} \qquad \begin{array}{r} 4 \\ + 9 \\ \hline \end{array} \qquad \begin{array}{r} 9 \\ + 8 \\ \hline \end{array} \qquad \begin{array}{r} 2 \\ + 9 \\ \hline \end{array} \qquad \begin{array}{r} 3 \\ + 9 \\ \hline \end{array}$$

$$\begin{array}{r} 9 \\ + 2 \\ \hline \end{array} \qquad \begin{array}{r} 6 \\ + 9 \\ \hline \end{array} \qquad \begin{array}{r} 7 \\ + 9 \\ \hline \end{array} \qquad \begin{array}{r} 9 \\ + 0 \\ \hline \end{array} \qquad \begin{array}{r} 8 \\ + 9 \\ \hline \end{array}$$

$$\begin{array}{r} 3 \\ + 9 \\ \hline \end{array} \qquad \begin{array}{r} 9 \\ + 4 \\ \hline \end{array} \qquad \begin{array}{r} 9 \\ + 6 \\ \hline \end{array} \qquad \begin{array}{r} 2 \\ + 9 \\ \hline \end{array} \qquad \begin{array}{r} 9 \\ + 9 \\ \hline \end{array}$$

$$\begin{array}{r} 9 \\ + 5 \\ \hline \end{array} \qquad \begin{array}{r} 0 \\ + 9 \\ \hline \end{array} \qquad \begin{array}{r} 5 \\ + 9 \\ \hline \end{array} \qquad \begin{array}{r} 9 \\ + 1 \\ \hline \end{array} \qquad \begin{array}{r} 9 \\ + 4 \\ \hline \end{array}$$

Score: _____

Name _____

Date _____

Draw a picture and write a number sentence for the story. Write the answer with a label.

1. Marcus had 40¢. His mother gave him 10¢. How much money does Marcus have now?

   ┌───┐
   │   │
   │   │
   │   │
   │   │
   │   │
   └───┘

   Number sentence _____

   Answer _____

2. Shade one fourth.   Shade three sixths.   Shade two eighths.

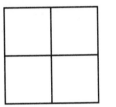   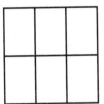

3. Use the favorite apple graph to answer these questions.

   How many children voted? _____

   What was the favorite apple? _____

   How many children chose that apple? _____

4. I have 3 dimes and 4 pennies. How much money is that? _____

   I have 5 tens and 6 ones. How much is that? _____

5. Find each sum.

$$\begin{array}{cc} 10 & 9 \\ +\ 4 & +\ 4 \\ \hline \end{array} \qquad \begin{array}{cc} 10 & 9 \\ +\ 7 & +\ 7 \\ \hline \end{array} \qquad \begin{array}{cc} 5 & 5 \\ +\ 10 & +\ 9 \\ \hline \end{array}$$

Name _____   **LESSON 42B**
                                                  Math 2
Date _____

Draw a picture and write a number sentence for the story. Write the answer with a label.

1.   Althea had 60¢. She spent 10¢. How much money does she have now?

┌───┐
│   │
│   │
│   │
│   │
└───┘

Number sentence _____

Answer _____

2.   Shade three fourths.   Shade one half.   Shade six eighths.

3.   Fill in the missing numbers.

5, 10, 15, _____, _____, _____, _____, _____, _____, _____

1, 3, 5, _____, _____, _____, _____, _____, _____, _____

4.   I have 2 dimes and 5 pennies. How much money is that? _____

I have 9 tens and 7 ones. How much is that? _____

5.   Find each sum.

$$
\begin{array}{cc}
10 & 9 \\
+\ 3 & +\ 3 \\
\hline
\end{array}
\qquad
\begin{array}{cc}
6 & 6 \\
+\ 10 & +\ 9 \\
\hline
\end{array}
\qquad
\begin{array}{cc}
10 & 9 \\
+\ 4 & +4 \\
\hline
\end{array}
$$

2-42Wb

4 + 3	4 + 5	2 + 8	6 + 6	6 + 5
7 + 6	3 + 7	5 + 4	2 + 7	5 + 1
4 + 6	3 + 4	1 + 9	8 + 2	5 + 5
3 + 3	6 + 2	8 + 9	7 + 3	2 + 0
3 + 7	0 + 5	4 + 4	7 + 8	1 + 8

Score: _____

2-43Fa

Name _____   **LESSON 43A**

Date _____   *Math 2*

Draw a picture and write a number sentence for this story. Write the answer with a label.

1. Anna has 1 ruler, 5 pencils, 2 notebooks, and 4 markers. How many of these things can she use to write with?

    Number sentence _____

    Answer _____

2. Draw a picture of the favorite apple graph your class made.

    _____

    _____

    _____

    What apple was chosen by the fewest number of children? _____

    How many children chose that apple? _____

3. How much money is 2 pennies and 6 dimes? _____

    How much is 5 ones and 3 tens? _____

4. Use the fewest number of dimes and pennies.

    3 dimes and 14 pennies = _____ dimes + _____ pennies = _____ ¢

5. Fill in the missing numbers on this piece of a hundred number chart.

		45		
			56	
	64			

Name _____   **LESSON 43B**

Date _____   *Math 2*

Draw a picture and write a number sentence for this story. Write the answer with a label.

1. Mike counted three cans of corn, four jars of beans, a package of napkins, and two jars of plant food on the shelf. How many containers of food are safe to eat?

[ ]

Number sentence _____

Answer _____

2. Fill in the missing addends.

$\boxed{} + 8 = 10$ $\qquad$ $\boxed{} + 4 = 9$ $\qquad$ $\boxed{} + 6 = 12$

$5 + \boxed{} = 7$ $\qquad$ $3 + \boxed{} = 3$ $\qquad$ $7 + \boxed{} = 8$

3. How much money is 3 pennies and 9 dimes? _____

How much is 6 ones and 2 tens? _____

4. Use the fewest number of dimes and pennies.

5 dimes and 12 pennies = _____ dimes + _____ pennies = _____ ¢

5. Fill in the missing numbers on this piece of a hundred number chart.

	73						
				86			
						98	

Object Weighed	Estimate	Actual

1 + 9	9 + 8	9 + 7	9 + 9	9 + 2
9 + 3	4 + 9	9 + 8	2 + 9	3 + 9
9 + 2	6 + 9	7 + 9	9 + 0	8 + 9
3 + 9	9 + 4	9 + 6	2 + 9	9 + 9
9 + 5	0 + 9	5 + 9	9 + 1	9 + 4

Score: _____

2-44Fa

Name _____

Date _____

Write a number sentence for the story. Write the answer with a label.

1. On Fridays, the children can buy pizza or hot dogs for lunch. Last Friday, eighty children bought pizza and ten children bought hot dogs. How many children bought lunch last Friday?

    Number sentence _____

    Answer _____

2. Divide the square in half using a vertical line segment.

    Divide the square in half using a horizontal line segment.

    Divide the square in half using an oblique line segment.

    Shade one half of each square.

3. How much money is 2 dimes and 6 pennies? _____

    How much money is 2 pennies and 6 dimes? _____

    Circle the one that is more.

4. Find each sum.

    $7 + 8 = $ _____ $5 + 6 = $ _____ $9 + 8$ _____

    $4 + 9 = $ _____ $5 + 9 = $ _____ $9 + 6$ _____

5. Count by 5's. Write the numbers.

    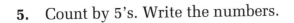

    5, _____, _____, _____, _____, _____, _____, _____, _____, _____

Name _____   **LESSON 44B**

Date _____   *Math 2*

Write a number sentence for the story. Write the answer with a label.

1. Crystal read the first 40 pages of the book on Saturday. On Sunday, she read 10 more pages. How many pages did she read altogether?

    Number sentence _____

    Answer _____

2. Divide the circle in   Divide the circle in   Divide the circle in
    half using a vertical   half using a horizontal   half using an oblique
    line segment.   line segment.   line segment.

    Shade one half of each circle.

3. How much money is 3 dimes and 5 pennies? _____

    How much money is 3 pennies and 5 dimes? _____

    Circle the one that is more.

4. Find each sum.

    $3 + 4 =$ _____ $6 + 7 =$ _____ $5 + 6 =$ _____

    $3 + 9 =$ _____ $5 + 9 =$ _____ $9 + 7 =$ _____

5. Count backwards by 5's. Write the numbers.

    50, _____, _____, _____, _____, _____, _____, _____, _____, _____

Name _____   **ASSESSMENT 8**

Date _____   **LESSON 45**

                                   Math 2

Draw a picture and write a number sentence for this story. Write the answer with a label.

1. Steven has four dimes. Mark has two dimes. How many dimes do they have together?

   [ ]

   Number sentence _____

   Answer _____

   How much money is that? _____

2. I have 7 dimes and 2 pennies. How much money is that? _____

   I have 3 tens and 8 ones. How much is that? _____

3. Count by 10's.

   __10__ , _____ , _____ , _____ , _____ , _____ , _____ , _____ , _____ , _____

   Count by 5's.

   __5__ , _____ , _____ , _____ , _____ , _____ , _____ , _____ , _____ , _____

4. Color the circle divided into fourths red.

   Color the circle divided into halves blue.

   Color the circle divided into eighths green.

5. Find the sums.

   $40 + 10 =$ _____ $10 + 80 =$ _____ $10 + 70 =$ _____

6. Fill in the missing addends.

   $\boxed{} + 7 = 10$ $4 + \boxed{} = 10$ $\boxed{} + 2 = 10$

10	2	6	18	12
− 5	− 1	− 3	− 9	− 6

16	8	4	14	10
− 8	− 4	− 2	− 7	− 5

8	2	16	6	12
− 4	− 1	− 8	− 3	− 6

4	10	18	8	12
− 2	− 5	− 9	− 4	− 6

14	16	2	6	14
− 7	− 8	− 1	− 3	− 7

Score: _____

Name _____ **LESSON 45A**

Math 2

Date _____

Draw a picture and write a number sentence for this story. Write the answer with a label.

1. Jay counted nine sharpened pencils and six unsharpened pencils in the pencil can. How many pencils are in the can?

Number sentence _____

Answer _____

2. How many mittens are in the box? _____
   Circle pairs of mittens.

   How many pairs of mittens are there? _____

   Count by 5's to find the number of fingers in all the mittens.

   _____ fingers

3. What is an even number greater than 6? _____

   What is an odd number less than 6? _____

4. Which number on the thermometer is the temperature closest to? _____ °F

5. How many dimes are there? _____ How many pennies are there? _____

   How much money is this? _____

Name _____   **LESSON 45B**
                                                           Math 2
Date _____

Draw a picture and write a number sentence for this story. Write the answer with a label.

1. Ferma has a set of 10 markers. She threw away 3 markers because they were dry.
    How many markers does she have now?

    +---+
    | |
    | |
    | |
    | |
    +---+

    Number sentence _____

    Answer _____

2. How many gloves are in the box? _____
    Circle pairs of gloves.

    How many pairs of gloves are there? _____

    Count by 5's to find the number of
    fingers in all the gloves.

                    _____ fingers

3. What is an even number less than 6? _____

    What is an odd number greater than 6? _____

4. Which number on the thermometer is the temperature closest to? _____ °F

5. How many dimes are there? _____   How many pennies are there? _____

    How much money is this? _____

Measure the line segments to the nearest inch.

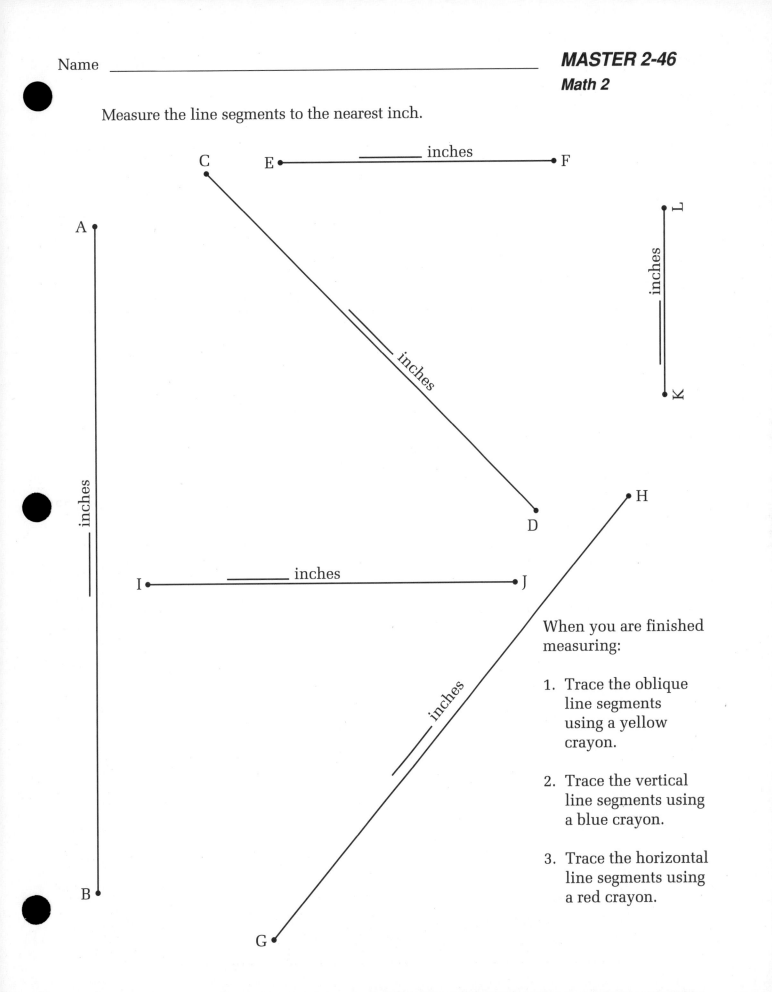

When you are finished measuring:

1. Trace the oblique line segments using a yellow crayon.

2. Trace the vertical line segments using a blue crayon.

3. Trace the horizontal line segments using a red crayon.

$$
\begin{array}{r} 1 \\ +\ 9 \\ \hline \end{array}
\qquad
\begin{array}{r} 9 \\ +\ 8 \\ \hline \end{array}
\qquad
\begin{array}{r} 9 \\ +\ 7 \\ \hline \end{array}
\qquad
\begin{array}{r} 9 \\ +\ 9 \\ \hline \end{array}
\qquad
\begin{array}{r} 9 \\ +\ 2 \\ \hline \end{array}
$$

$$
\begin{array}{r} 9 \\ +\ 3 \\ \hline \end{array}
\qquad
\begin{array}{r} 4 \\ +\ 9 \\ \hline \end{array}
\qquad
\begin{array}{r} 9 \\ +\ 8 \\ \hline \end{array}
\qquad
\begin{array}{r} 2 \\ +\ 9 \\ \hline \end{array}
\qquad
\begin{array}{r} 3 \\ +\ 9 \\ \hline \end{array}
$$

$$
\begin{array}{r} 9 \\ +\ 2 \\ \hline \end{array}
\qquad
\begin{array}{r} 6 \\ +\ 9 \\ \hline \end{array}
\qquad
\begin{array}{r} 7 \\ +\ 9 \\ \hline \end{array}
\qquad
\begin{array}{r} 9 \\ +\ 0 \\ \hline \end{array}
\qquad
\begin{array}{r} 8 \\ +\ 9 \\ \hline \end{array}
$$

$$
\begin{array}{r} 3 \\ +\ 9 \\ \hline \end{array}
\qquad
\begin{array}{r} 9 \\ +\ 4 \\ \hline \end{array}
\qquad
\begin{array}{r} 9 \\ +\ 6 \\ \hline \end{array}
\qquad
\begin{array}{r} 2 \\ +\ 9 \\ \hline \end{array}
\qquad
\begin{array}{r} 9 \\ +\ 9 \\ \hline \end{array}
$$

$$
\begin{array}{r} 9 \\ +\ 5 \\ \hline \end{array}
\qquad
\begin{array}{r} 0 \\ +\ 9 \\ \hline \end{array}
\qquad
\begin{array}{r} 5 \\ +\ 9 \\ \hline \end{array}
\qquad
\begin{array}{r} 9 \\ +\ 1 \\ \hline \end{array}
\qquad
\begin{array}{r} 9 \\ +\ 4 \\ \hline \end{array}
$$

Score: _____

Name _____   **LESSON 46A**

● Date _____   *Math 2*

Draw a picture and write a number sentence for this story. Write the answer with a label.

1. Amy's dog had 8 puppies. She gave five puppies to her friends and one to her grandmother. How many puppies does Amy have now?

   ┌──┐
   │   │
   │   │
   │   │
   │   │
   │   │
   └──┘

   Number sentence _____

   Answer _____

2. Measure this line segment using inches.

   ●━━━━━━━━━━━━━━━━━━━━━━━━━━●   _____ "

● 3. Fill in the missing numbers. Use the fewest possible number of pennies.

   3 dimes and 16 pennies = _____ dimes + _____ pennies = _____ ¢

4. I have 4 pennies and 9 dimes. How much money is that? _____

   I have 6 ones and 7 tens. How much is that? _____

5. Write the digital time.

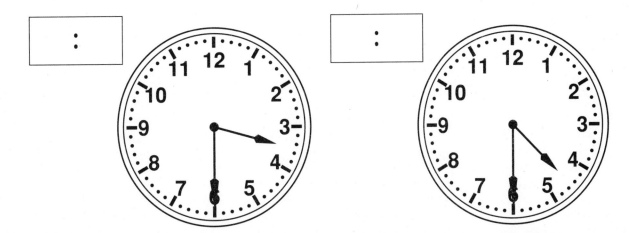

●

Name _____

Date _____

Draw a picture and write a number sentence for this story. Write the answer with a label.

1. Beth's cat had 5 kittens. She gave 2 kittens to her teacher and one to her aunt. How many kittens does Beth have now?

Number sentence _____

Answer _____

2. This is a six-inch line segment. Find something at home that is 6" long.

What did you find? _____

3. Fill in the missing numbers. Use the fewest possible number of pennies.

   5 dimes and 12 pennies = _____ dimes + _____ pennies = _____ ¢

4. I have 9 pennies and 4 dimes. How much money is that? _____

   I have 7 ones and 6 tens. How much is that? _____

5. Write the digital time.

2-46Wb

4 + 3	4 + 5	2 + 8	6 + 6	6 + 5
7 + 6	3 + 7	5 + 4	2 + 7	5 + 1
4 + 6	3 + 4	1 + 9	8 + 2	5 + 5
3 + 3	6 + 2	8 + 9	7 + 3	2 + 0
3 + 7	0 + 5	4 + 4	7 + 8	1 + 8

Score: _____

Name _____

Date _____

Write a number sentence for this story. Write the answer with a label.

1. Stuart has 10 large marbles and 24 small marbles. How many marbles does he have?

    Number sentence _____

    Answer _____

2. Measure this line segment to the nearest inch.

    ●————————————————————————● _____"

3. Fill in the missing numbers. Use the fewest possible number of pennies.

    4 dimes and 17 pennies = _____ dimes + _____ pennies = _____¢

4. Color one half using a blue crayon.

    Color one fourth using a red crayon.

    Color one eighth using a green crayon.

    Color one sixth using a purple crayon.

5. Find each sum.

    36 + 10 = _____   28 + 10 = _____

    10 + 42 = _____   73 + 10 = _____

6. Fill in the missing numbers on this piece of a hundred number chart.

	63			
		85		

Name _____   **LESSON 47B**
                                                   Math 2
Date _____

Write a number sentence for this story. Write the answer with a label.

1. Clara had 35 pennies. Her brother gave her 10 more pennies. How many pennies does she have now?

    Number sentence _____

    Answer _____

2. Which number on the thermometer is the temperature closest to? _____°F

3. Fill in the missing numbers. Use the fewest possible number of pennies.

    6 dimes and 18 pennies = _____ dimes + _____ pennies = _____ ¢

4. Color one half using a blue crayon.

    Color one fourth using an orange crayon.

    Color one eighth using a red crayon.

    Color one third using a green crayon.

5. Find each sum.

    85 + 10 = ____   10 + 37 = ____

    29 + 10 = ____   10 + 21 = ____

6. Fill in the missing numbers on this piece of a hundred number chart.

	24			
		45		

Name _____

A 7.1

$$\begin{array}{r} 1 \\ + 9 \\ \hline \end{array} \qquad \begin{array}{r} 9 \\ + 8 \\ \hline \end{array} \qquad \begin{array}{r} 9 \\ + 7 \\ \hline \end{array} \qquad \begin{array}{r} 9 \\ + 9 \\ \hline \end{array} \qquad \begin{array}{r} 9 \\ + 2 \\ \hline \end{array}$$

$$\begin{array}{r} 9 \\ + 3 \\ \hline \end{array} \qquad \begin{array}{r} 4 \\ + 9 \\ \hline \end{array} \qquad \begin{array}{r} 9 \\ + 8 \\ \hline \end{array} \qquad \begin{array}{r} 2 \\ + 9 \\ \hline \end{array} \qquad \begin{array}{r} 3 \\ + 9 \\ \hline \end{array}$$

$$\begin{array}{r} 9 \\ + 2 \\ \hline \end{array} \qquad \begin{array}{r} 6 \\ + 9 \\ \hline \end{array} \qquad \begin{array}{r} 7 \\ + 9 \\ \hline \end{array} \qquad \begin{array}{r} 9 \\ + 0 \\ \hline \end{array} \qquad \begin{array}{r} 8 \\ + 9 \\ \hline \end{array}$$

$$\begin{array}{r} 3 \\ + 9 \\ \hline \end{array} \qquad \begin{array}{r} 9 \\ + 4 \\ \hline \end{array} \qquad \begin{array}{r} 9 \\ + 6 \\ \hline \end{array} \qquad \begin{array}{r} 2 \\ + 9 \\ \hline \end{array} \qquad \begin{array}{r} 9 \\ + 9 \\ \hline \end{array}$$

$$\begin{array}{r} 9 \\ + 5 \\ \hline \end{array} \qquad \begin{array}{r} 0 \\ + 9 \\ \hline \end{array} \qquad \begin{array}{r} 5 \\ + 9 \\ \hline \end{array} \qquad \begin{array}{r} 9 \\ + 1 \\ \hline \end{array} \qquad \begin{array}{r} 9 \\ + 4 \\ \hline \end{array}$$

Score: _____

2-48Fa

Name _____   **LESSON 48A**

Math 2

Date _____

Write a number sentence for the story. Write the answer with a label.

1. The children in Room 2 collected 83 cans of food for the food drive. Ms. Roman brought in 10 more cans of food. How many cans of food did they collect?

    Number sentence _____

    Answer _____

2. Measure each line segment using inches.

    How long is the horizontal line segment? _____ "

    How long is the vertical line segment? _____ "

3. How much money is this? _____

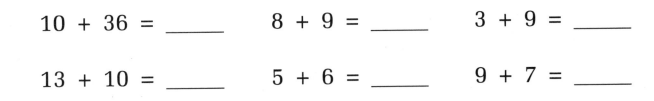

4. Chris has nine white socks.
    Draw the socks and circle the pairs.

    How many pairs are there? _____

    How many extras are there? _____

5. Find each sum.

    10 + 36 = ____   8 + 9 = ____   3 + 9 = ____

    13 + 10 = ____   5 + 6 = ____   9 + 7 = ____

Name _____

Date _____

Write a number sentence for the story. Write the answer with a label.

1. Ten children voted yes and 31 children voted no. How many children voted?

    Number sentence _____

    Answer _____

2. Color the fifth triangle blue.
    Color the sixth triangle red.
    Color the middle triangle yellow.

3. How much money is this? _____

4. Missy has seven white socks.
    Draw the socks and circle the pairs.

    How many pairs are there? _____

    How many extras are there? _____

5. Find each sum.

    10 + 43 = _____   6 + 7 = _____   4 + 9 = _____

    16 + 10 = _____   5 + 4 = _____   9 + 6 = _____

7	3	8	5	4
− 1	− 1	− 1	− 1	− 1
10	6	4	3	9
− 1	− 1	− 1	− 1	− 1
2	8	5	9	6
− 1	− 1	− 1	− 1	− 1
7	2	8	3	5
− 1	− 1	− 1	− 1	− 1
6	4	9	2	8
− 1	− 1	− 1	− 1	− 1

Score: _____

2-49Fa

1. Steven had 6 nickels. Michelle gave him 2 more nickels. Write a number sentence to show how many nickels he has now.

   Number sentence _____

   Answer _____   How much money is that? _____

2. Measure each line segment using inches.

   horizontal line segment _____

   oblique line segment _____

   vertical line segment _____

3. What is the fifth day of the week? _____

   What is the second day of the week? _____

   What is the seventh day of the week? _____

4. Number the clock face.
   Show half past five on the clock face.

   Write the digital time one hour from now.

5. Find each answer.

   $26 + 10 =$ _____ $10 + 72 =$ _____ $7 + 8 =$ _____

   $6 - 6 =$ _____ $9 + 5 =$ _____ $50 + 10 =$ _____

Name _____

Date _____

1. Marsha and Sandy are saving nickels. Marsha has 3 nickels and Sandy has 7 nickels. Write a number sentence to show how many nickels they have.

    Number sentence _____

    Answer _____   How much money is that? _____

2. Finish the number patterns.

    85, 84, 83, _____ , _____ , _____ , _____ , _____ , _____ , _____

    1, 3, 5, _____ , _____ , _____ , _____ , _____ , _____ , _____

    2, 4, 6, _____ , _____ , _____ , _____ , _____ , _____ , _____

    100, 90, 80, _____ , _____ , _____ , _____ , _____ , _____ , _____

3. Write the letter **E** in the fourth square.
    Write the letter **F** in the first square.
    Write the letter **D** in the sixth square.
    Write the letter **I** in the third square.
    Write the letter **N** in the fifth square.
    Write the letter **R** in the second square.

4. Number the clock face.
    Show half past nine on the clock face.

    Write the digital time one hour from now.

5. Find each answer.

    $39 + 10 =$ _____ $6 + 9 =$ _____ $30 + 10 =$ _____

    $5 - 5 =$ _____ $9 + 8 =$ _____ $10 + 19 =$ _____

2-49Wb

Name _____

Date _____

Draw a picture and write a number sentence for the story. Write the answer with a label.

1. Christa had 8 markers and 3 pencils. She gave 2 markers to her friend. How many markers does she have now?

    ┌───┐
    │   │
    │   │
    │   │
    │   │
    └───┘

    Number sentence _____

    Answer _____

2. Use a **yellow** crayon to trace the **oblique** line segment.
    Use a **red** crayon to trace the **horizontal** line segment.
    Use a **blue** crayon to trace the **vertical** line segment.

3. I have 4 pennies and 8 dimes. How much money is this? _____

    I have 9 tens and 3 ones. How much is that? _____

4. How many shoes are there? _____

    Circle pairs of shoes.

    How many pairs of shoes are there? _____

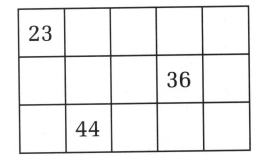

5. Fill in the missing numbers on this piece of a hundred number chart.

23				
			36	
	44			

6. Add.

    $5 + 9 =$ _____ $9 + 3 =$ _____ $7 + 9 =$ _____ $9 + 4 =$ _____

Name _____

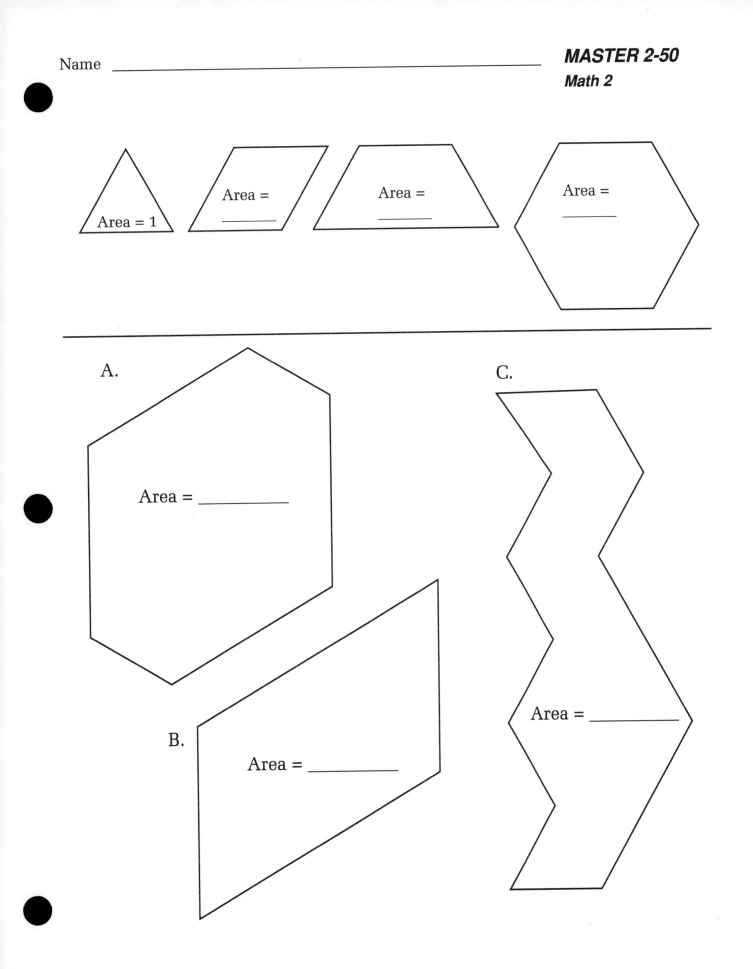

Area = 1

Area = _____

Area = _____

Area = _____

A.

Area = _____

B.

Area = _____

C.

Area = _____

Name _____

$$\begin{array}{r} 4 \\ -4 \\ \hline \end{array} \quad \begin{array}{r} 5 \\ -0 \\ \hline \end{array} \quad \begin{array}{r} 9 \\ -0 \\ \hline \end{array} \quad \begin{array}{r} 6 \\ -6 \\ \hline \end{array} \quad \begin{array}{r} 5 \\ -5 \\ \hline \end{array}$$

$$\begin{array}{r} 7 \\ -7 \\ \hline \end{array} \quad \begin{array}{r} 6 \\ -0 \\ \hline \end{array} \quad \begin{array}{r} 1 \\ -1 \\ \hline \end{array} \quad \begin{array}{r} 10 \\ -0 \\ \hline \end{array} \quad \begin{array}{r} 4 \\ -0 \\ \hline \end{array}$$

$$\begin{array}{r} 6 \\ -0 \\ \hline \end{array} \quad \begin{array}{r} 8 \\ -8 \\ \hline \end{array} \quad \begin{array}{r} 4 \\ -4 \\ \hline \end{array} \quad \begin{array}{r} 3 \\ -0 \\ \hline \end{array} \quad \begin{array}{r} 2 \\ -2 \\ \hline \end{array}$$

$$\begin{array}{r} 1 \\ -0 \\ \hline \end{array} \quad \begin{array}{r} 3 \\ -3 \\ \hline \end{array} \quad \begin{array}{r} 2 \\ -0 \\ \hline \end{array} \quad \begin{array}{r} 9 \\ -9 \\ \hline \end{array} \quad \begin{array}{r} 8 \\ -0 \\ \hline \end{array}$$

$$\begin{array}{r} 10 \\ -10 \\ \hline \end{array} \quad \begin{array}{r} 7 \\ -0 \\ \hline \end{array} \quad \begin{array}{r} 9 \\ -0 \\ \hline \end{array} \quad \begin{array}{r} 5 \\ -5 \\ \hline \end{array} \quad \begin{array}{r} 1 \\ -0 \\ \hline \end{array}$$

Score: _____

$$\begin{array}{r} 1 \\ + 9 \\ \hline \end{array} \qquad \begin{array}{r} 9 \\ + 8 \\ \hline \end{array} \qquad \begin{array}{r} 9 \\ + 7 \\ \hline \end{array} \qquad \begin{array}{r} 9 \\ + 9 \\ \hline \end{array} \qquad \begin{array}{r} 9 \\ + 2 \\ \hline \end{array}$$

$$\begin{array}{r} 9 \\ + 3 \\ \hline \end{array} \qquad \begin{array}{r} 4 \\ + 9 \\ \hline \end{array} \qquad \begin{array}{r} 9 \\ + 8 \\ \hline \end{array} \qquad \begin{array}{r} 2 \\ + 9 \\ \hline \end{array} \qquad \begin{array}{r} 3 \\ + 9 \\ \hline \end{array}$$

$$\begin{array}{r} 9 \\ + 2 \\ \hline \end{array} \qquad \begin{array}{r} 6 \\ + 9 \\ \hline \end{array} \qquad \begin{array}{r} 7 \\ + 9 \\ \hline \end{array} \qquad \begin{array}{r} 9 \\ + 0 \\ \hline \end{array} \qquad \begin{array}{r} 8 \\ + 9 \\ \hline \end{array}$$

$$\begin{array}{r} 3 \\ + 9 \\ \hline \end{array} \qquad \begin{array}{r} 9 \\ + 4 \\ \hline \end{array} \qquad \begin{array}{r} 9 \\ + 6 \\ \hline \end{array} \qquad \begin{array}{r} 2 \\ + 9 \\ \hline \end{array} \qquad \begin{array}{r} 9 \\ + 9 \\ \hline \end{array}$$

$$\begin{array}{r} 9 \\ + 5 \\ \hline \end{array} \qquad \begin{array}{r} 0 \\ + 9 \\ \hline \end{array} \qquad \begin{array}{r} 5 \\ + 9 \\ \hline \end{array} \qquad \begin{array}{r} 9 \\ + 1 \\ \hline \end{array} \qquad \begin{array}{r} 9 \\ + 4 \\ \hline \end{array}$$

Score: _____

Name _____

Date _____

Write a number sentence for the story. Write the answer with a label.

1. Susan had 12 pencils. Marsha gave Susan two pencils. How many pencils does Susan have now?

    Number sentence _____

    Answer _____

2. How much money is in each pocket?

    _____   _____   _____

    Circle the pocket with the most money.

3. Show **18** using tally marks.

    ┌───┐
    │   │
    │   │
    └───┘

4. One of these socks is my favorite sock.
    Use the clues to find my favorite sock.
    It is not the sock with the triangles.
    It is not the sock with the vertical lines.
    It is not first.
    It is not fourth.
    Circle my favorite sock.

5. Six children in Miss Wood's class graphed their tags.

    How many families have boys? _____

    How many families have only girls? _____

    How many families have both boys and girls? _____

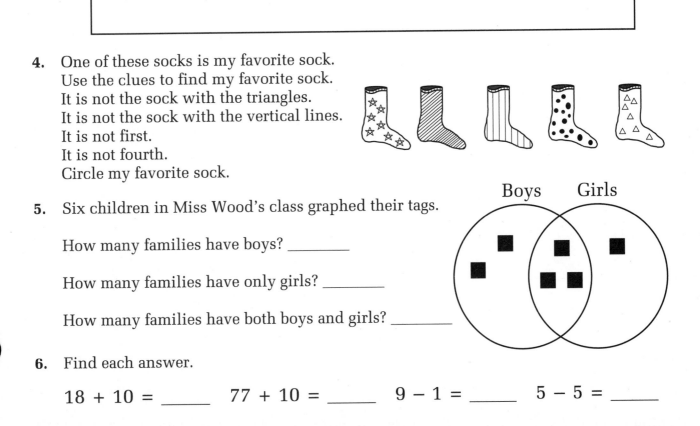

6. Find each answer.

    $18 + 10 =$ _____ $77 + 10 =$ _____ $9 - 1 =$ _____ $5 - 5 =$ _____

Name _____ **LESSON 51B**

Date _____ *Math 2*

Write a number sentence for the story. Write the answer with a label.

1. Miss Allen had 6 games. Miss Allen gave Mrs. Paolino's class 3 games to use. How many games does Miss Allen have now?

   Number sentence _____

   Answer _____

2. How much money is in each pocket?

   7 nickels   3 dimes   18 pennies

   _____   _____   _____

   Circle the pocket with the most money.

3. Show **31** using tally marks.

   | |
   | |
   | |

4. One of these socks is my sister's favorite sock.
   Use the clues to find her favorite sock.
   It is not the sock with the triangles.
   It is not the sock with the vertical lines.
   It is not first.
   It is not second.
   Circle my sister's favorite sock.

5. Eight children in Miss Gen's class graphed their tags.

   How many families have girls? _____

   How many families have only boys? _____

   How many families have both boys and girls? _____

   Boys   Girls

6. Find each answer.

   26 + 10 = _____   86 + 10 = _____   7 − 1 = _____   3 − 0 = _____

Name _____

$$\begin{array}{r} 5 \\ +1 \\ \hline \end{array} \quad \begin{array}{r} 8 \\ +9 \\ \hline \end{array} \quad \begin{array}{r} 9 \\ +5 \\ \hline \end{array} \quad \begin{array}{r} 5 \\ +5 \\ \hline \end{array} \quad \begin{array}{r} 9 \\ +4 \\ \hline \end{array}$$

$$\begin{array}{r} 9 \\ +9 \\ \hline \end{array} \quad \begin{array}{r} 2 \\ +9 \\ \hline \end{array} \quad \begin{array}{r} 7 \\ +2 \\ \hline \end{array} \quad \begin{array}{r} 3 \\ +7 \\ \hline \end{array} \quad \begin{array}{r} 7 \\ +7 \\ \hline \end{array}$$

$$\begin{array}{r} 5 \\ +4 \\ \hline \end{array} \quad \begin{array}{r} 4 \\ +6 \\ \hline \end{array} \quad \begin{array}{r} 3 \\ +3 \\ \hline \end{array} \quad \begin{array}{r} 4 \\ +3 \\ \hline \end{array} \quad \begin{array}{r} 8 \\ +2 \\ \hline \end{array}$$

$$\begin{array}{r} 6 \\ +6 \\ \hline \end{array} \quad \begin{array}{r} 7 \\ +8 \\ \hline \end{array} \quad \begin{array}{r} 9 \\ +0 \\ \hline \end{array} \quad \begin{array}{r} 5 \\ +9 \\ \hline \end{array} \quad \begin{array}{r} 3 \\ +9 \\ \hline \end{array}$$

$$\begin{array}{r} 3 \\ +7 \\ \hline \end{array} \quad \begin{array}{r} 4 \\ +9 \\ \hline \end{array} \quad \begin{array}{r} 0 \\ +5 \\ \hline \end{array} \quad \begin{array}{r} 8 \\ +8 \\ \hline \end{array} \quad \begin{array}{r} 9 \\ +6 \\ \hline \end{array}$$

Score: _____

Name _____

Date _____

Write a number sentence for the story. Write the answer with a label.

1. Nathan has 8 pencils in his desk. Keith has 7 pencils in his desk. How many pencils do they have together?

   Number sentence _____

   Answer _____

2. Measure each side of this square.

3. Divide the square into fourths. Shade one fourth.

4. How much money is this? _____

5. Draw a line of symmetry for each shape.

6. Circle the number that is 1 more than **35**.
   Put an X on the number that is 1 less than **47**.

14	34
46	45
36	48

Name _____   **LESSON 52B**

Date _____   *Math 2*

Write a number sentence for the story. Write the answer with a label.

1. Beth had twelve books. She gave one to her brother. How many books does she have now?

    Number sentence _____

    Answer _____

2. Divide the square into eighths.
    Shade seven eighths.

3. Finish the number patterns.

    10, 20, 30, ____, ____, ____, ____, ____, ____, ____

    50, 55, 60, 65, ____, ____, ____, ____, ____, ____, ____

4. How much money is this? _____

5. Draw a line of symmetry for each shape.

6. Circle the number that is 1 more than **42**.
    Put an X on the number that is 1 less than **54**.

55	41
42	53
43	54

Name _____

S 2.0

7	3	8	5	4
− 1	− 1	− 1	− 1	− 1

10	6	4	3	9
− 1	− 1	− 1	− 1	− 1

2	8	5	9	6
− 1	− 1	− 1	− 1	− 1

7	2	8	3	5
− 1	− 1	− 1	− 1	− 1

6	4	9	2	8
− 1	− 1	− 1	− 1	− 1

Score: _____

2-53Fa

Name _____

Date _____

Write a number sentence for the story. Write the answer with a label.

1. Mrs. Hannan's classroom has 32 pairs of right-handed scissors and 10 pairs of left-handed scissors. How many pairs of scissors are there in all?

    Number sentence _____

    Answer _____

2. Draw a line of symmetry for each letter.

    # M O D

3. How much money is this? _____

4. How many earrings are there? _____

    Circle the pairs.

    How many pairs of earrings are there? _____

5. Find each answer.

    78 + 10 = _____   35 − 10 = _____   23 + 10 = _____

    30 − 10 = _____   60 + 10 = _____   62 − 10 = _____

6. What time is shown on the clock?

    [:]

    What time will it be one hour later?

    [:]

Name _____

Date _____

Math 2

Write a number sentence for the story. Write the answer with a label.

1. Ryan had 64 baseball cards. His brother gave him 10 more cards. How many cards does he have now?

Number sentence _____

Answer _____

2. Draw a line of symmetry for each letter.

H   V   X

3. How much money is this? _____

4. Draw 12 shoes.

Circle the pairs.

How many pairs of shoes are there? _____

5. Find each answer.

65 + 10 = _____   57 − 10 = _____   37 + 10 = _____

40 − 10 = _____   20 + 10 = _____   84 − 10 = _____

6. What time is shown on the clock?

> :

What time will it be one hour later?

> :

2-53Wb

Copyright by Saxon Publishers, Inc. and Nancy Larson. Reproduction prohibited.

$$
\begin{array}{r} 4 \\ -\ 4 \\ \hline \end{array}
\qquad
\begin{array}{r} 5 \\ -\ 0 \\ \hline \end{array}
\qquad
\begin{array}{r} 9 \\ -\ 0 \\ \hline \end{array}
\qquad
\begin{array}{r} 6 \\ -\ 6 \\ \hline \end{array}
\qquad
\begin{array}{r} 5 \\ -\ 5 \\ \hline \end{array}
$$

$$
\begin{array}{r} 7 \\ -\ 7 \\ \hline \end{array}
\qquad
\begin{array}{r} 6 \\ -\ 0 \\ \hline \end{array}
\qquad
\begin{array}{r} 1 \\ -\ 1 \\ \hline \end{array}
\qquad
\begin{array}{r} 10 \\ -\ 0 \\ \hline \end{array}
\qquad
\begin{array}{r} 4 \\ -\ 0 \\ \hline \end{array}
$$

$$
\begin{array}{r} 6 \\ -\ 0 \\ \hline \end{array}
\qquad
\begin{array}{r} 8 \\ -\ 8 \\ \hline \end{array}
\qquad
\begin{array}{r} 4 \\ -\ 4 \\ \hline \end{array}
\qquad
\begin{array}{r} 3 \\ -\ 0 \\ \hline \end{array}
\qquad
\begin{array}{r} 2 \\ -\ 2 \\ \hline \end{array}
$$

$$
\begin{array}{r} 1 \\ -\ 0 \\ \hline \end{array}
\qquad
\begin{array}{r} 3 \\ -\ 3 \\ \hline \end{array}
\qquad
\begin{array}{r} 2 \\ -\ 0 \\ \hline \end{array}
\qquad
\begin{array}{r} 9 \\ -\ 9 \\ \hline \end{array}
\qquad
\begin{array}{r} 8 \\ -\ 0 \\ \hline \end{array}
$$

$$
\begin{array}{r} 10 \\ -\ 10 \\ \hline \end{array}
\qquad
\begin{array}{r} 7 \\ -\ 0 \\ \hline \end{array}
\qquad
\begin{array}{r} 9 \\ -\ 0 \\ \hline \end{array}
\qquad
\begin{array}{r} 5 \\ -\ 5 \\ \hline \end{array}
\qquad
\begin{array}{r} 1 \\ -\ 0 \\ \hline \end{array}
$$

Score: _____

Name _____   **LESSON 54A**

Date _____   *Math 2*

Write a number sentence for the story. Write the answer with a label.

1. Weston had 60¢. His sister gave him ten cents. How much money does he have now?

   What kind of problem is this? _____

   Number sentence _____ Answer _____

2. Circle the largest number.

   Put an X on the smallest number.

   Write the numbers in order from smallest to largest.

   | 52 | 38 | 21 |

   _____   _____   _____

   smallest   largest

3.

   How many dimes are there? _____   How much money is that? _____

   How many nickels are there? _____   How much money is that? _____

   How many pennies are there? _____   How much money is that? _____

4. Find each answer.

   $55 + 10 =$ _____ $27 + 10 =$ _____ $40 - 10 =$ _____

   $64 - 10 =$ _____ $51 - 10 =$ _____ $70 + 10 =$ _____

5. Measure this line segment using inches.

   ●━━━━━━━━━━━━━━━●   _____ "

Name _____   **LESSON 54B**
                                                  Math 2
Date _____

Write a number sentence for the story. Write the answer with a label.

1. Stephen had 50¢. He gave his sister ten cents. How much money does he have now?

    What kind of problem is this? _____

    Number sentence _____ Answer _____

2. Circle the largest number.
    Put an X on the smallest number.
    Write the numbers in order from smallest to largest.

    | 49   73   61 |

    _____   _____   _____
       smallest   largest

3. Ask your mom or dad to let you count the change they have in their pocket or purse.
    (Don't count the quarters.)

    How many dimes are there? _____   How much money is that? _____

    How many nickels are there? _____   How much money is that? _____

    How many pennies are there? _____   How much money is that? _____

4. Find each answer.

    24 − 10 = _____   46 + 10 = _____   61 − 10 = _____

    50 + 10 = _____   70 − 10 = _____   82 + 10 = _____

5. Finish the number patterns.

    5, 10, 15, _____, _____, _____, _____, _____, _____, _____

    1, 3, 5, _____, _____, _____, _____, _____, _____, _____

    56, 57, 58, _____, _____, _____, _____, _____, _____, _____

Name _____

Date _____

Write a number sentence for the story. Write the answer with a label.

1. Courtney had a box of 64 crayons. She gave Sharon 10 crayons. How many crayons does Courtney have now?

   Number sentence _____

   Answer _____

2. One of these is my favorite color.
   Use the clues to find my favorite color.

   | blue   yellow   red   green   purple |

   It is not in the middle.
   It does not have four letters.
   It is not fifth.
   It is not second.
   Circle my favorite color.

3. What number on the thermometer is the temperature closest to? _____°F

4. Measure each line segment using inches.

   •———————————————————• _____ "

   •————————————• _____ "

5. Finish the patterns.

   2, 4, 6, _____, _____, _____, _____, _____, _____, _____

   1, 3, 5, _____, _____, _____, _____, _____, _____, _____

6. Find each answer.

   46 + 10 = _____   10 + 37 = _____   74 + 10 = _____

2-55Aa

5 + 1	8 + 9	9 + 5	5 + 5	9 + 4
9 + 9	2 + 9	7 + 2	3 + 7	7 + 7
5 + 4	4 + 6	3 + 3	4 + 3	8 + 2
6 + 6	7 + 8	9 + 0	5 + 9	3 + 9
3 + 7	4 + 9	0 + 5	8 + 8	9 + 6

Score: _____

Name _____

Date _____

Write a number sentence for the story. Write the answer with a label.

1. Sean ironed five shirts in the morning. In the afternoon he ironed ten more shirts. How many shirts did he iron altogether?

    Number sentence _____

    Answer _____

2. Circle the largest number.
    Put an X on the smallest number.
    Write the numbers in order from smallest to largest.

    | 52 | 21 | 57 |

    _____   _____   _____
    smallest   largest

3. Number the number line.
    Put a point at **3**. Label it **N**.
    Put a point at **5**. Label it **D**.

    ←——+———+———+———+———+———+———+———→
         0

4. Which number on the thermometer is the temperature closest to?

    _____°F

5. Draw 4 pairs of mittens. Circle the pairs.

    How many fingers will be in the mittens? _____

    Show that number using tally marks.

100°
90°
80°
70°
60°
50°
40°
30°
20°
10°
0°
−10°
−20°

Name _____   **LESSON 55B**
                                          Math 2
Date _____

Write a number sentence for the story. Write the answer with a label.

1. Ivan's dog ate 9 dog biscuits on Sunday. On Monday he ate 10 more. How many dog biscuits did he eat altogether?

    Number sentence _____

    Answer _____

2. Circle the largest number.
    Put an X on the smallest number.
    Write the numbers in order from smallest to largest.

    | 75   46   43 |

    _____   _____   _____
         smallest   largest

3. Number the number line.
    Put a point at **4**. Label it **P**.
    Put a point at **1**. Label it **T**.

    ←——+——+——+——+——+——+——+——+——→
        0

4. Which number on the thermometer is the temperature closest to?

    _____°F

5. Draw 3 pairs of socks. Circle the pairs.

    [ ]

    How many toes will be in the socks? _____

    Show that number using tally marks.

    [ ]

100°
90°
80°
70°
60°
50°
40°
30°
20°
10°
0°
−10°
−20°

What we measured	_____'s feet	_____'s feet	ruler feet

$$
\begin{array}{r} 5 \\ -\ 0 \\ \hline \end{array}
\qquad
\begin{array}{r} 6 \\ -\ 6 \\ \hline \end{array}
\qquad
\begin{array}{r} 10 \\ -\ 5 \\ \hline \end{array}
\qquad
\begin{array}{r} 1 \\ -\ 0 \\ \hline \end{array}
\qquad
\begin{array}{r} 7 \\ -\ 1 \\ \hline \end{array}
$$

$$
\begin{array}{r} 14 \\ -\ 7 \\ \hline \end{array}
\qquad
\begin{array}{r} 5 \\ -\ 1 \\ \hline \end{array}
\qquad
\begin{array}{r} 7 \\ -\ 0 \\ \hline \end{array}
\qquad
\begin{array}{r} 4 \\ -\ 2 \\ \hline \end{array}
\qquad
\begin{array}{r} 9 \\ -\ 9 \\ \hline \end{array}
$$

$$
\begin{array}{r} 9 \\ -\ 1 \\ \hline \end{array}
\qquad
\begin{array}{r} 8 \\ -\ 0 \\ \hline \end{array}
\qquad
\begin{array}{r} 18 \\ -\ 9 \\ \hline \end{array}
\qquad
\begin{array}{r} 3 \\ -\ 3 \\ \hline \end{array}
\qquad
\begin{array}{r} 2 \\ -\ 0 \\ \hline \end{array}
$$

$$
\begin{array}{r} 16 \\ -\ 8 \\ \hline \end{array}
\qquad
\begin{array}{r} 3 \\ -\ 1 \\ \hline \end{array}
\qquad
\begin{array}{r} 5 \\ -\ 5 \\ \hline \end{array}
\qquad
\begin{array}{r} 6 \\ -\ 0 \\ \hline \end{array}
\qquad
\begin{array}{r} 12 \\ -\ 6 \\ \hline \end{array}
$$

$$
\begin{array}{r} 6 \\ -\ 1 \\ \hline \end{array}
\qquad
\begin{array}{r} 9 \\ -\ 0 \\ \hline \end{array}
\qquad
\begin{array}{r} 6 \\ -\ 3 \\ \hline \end{array}
\qquad
\begin{array}{r} 8 \\ -\ 8 \\ \hline \end{array}
\qquad
\begin{array}{r} 4 \\ -\ 1 \\ \hline \end{array}
$$

Score: _____

Name _____

Date _____

Write a number sentence for the story. Write the answer with a label.

1. There were 25 children in Room 12. Ten children left to go to the library. How many children are in Room 12 now?

    Number sentence _____

    Answer _____

2. Number the number line.
    Put a point at **4**. Label it **P**.
    Put a point at **1**. Label it **T**.

    Where is point **Z**? _____

3. Fill in the missing numbers on this piece of a hundred number chart.

	37		
46			49

4. Color the even numbers in Problem 3 red.
    Color the odd numbers in Problem 3 yellow.

5. Fill in the missing numbers. Use the fewest number of pennies possible.

    7 dimes + 11 pennies = _____ dimes + _____ pennies = _____¢

    3 dimes + 19 pennies = _____ dimes + _____ pennies = _____¢

6. Find each answer.

    $58 - 10 =$ _____ $92 - 10 =$ _____ $18 - 10 =$ _____

    $40 + 10 =$ _____ $35 + 10 =$ _____ $50 - 10 =$ _____

Name _____

Date _____

Write a number sentence for the story. Write the answer with a label.

1. Sarah had 65¢. She gave her brother a dime. How much money does she have now?

    Number sentence _____

    Answer _____

2. Number the number line.
   Put a point at **5**. Label it **A**.
   Put a point at **3**. Label it **B**.

   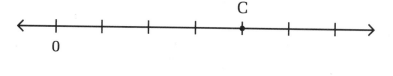

   Where is point **C**? _____

3. Fill in the missing numbers on this piece of a hundred number chart.

		74				
82						
	95					

4. Use your feet to measure the length of your bedroom.
   (Walk in a straight line.)   _____ feet

   Have someone else in your family measure your bedroom with their feet.
   Name _____   _____ feet
   Who took more steps? _____
   Why? _____

5. Fill in the missing numbers. Use the fewest number of pennies possible.

   2 dimes + 16 pennies = _____ dimes + _____ pennies = _____ ¢

6. Find each answer.

   63 − 10 = _____   80 + 10 = _____   17 + 10 = _____

   24 + 10 = _____   26 − 10 = _____   32 − 10 = _____

2-56Wb

$$
\begin{array}{r}5\\+1\\\hline\end{array}\qquad
\begin{array}{r}8\\+9\\\hline\end{array}\qquad
\begin{array}{r}9\\+5\\\hline\end{array}\qquad
\begin{array}{r}5\\+5\\\hline\end{array}\qquad
\begin{array}{r}9\\+4\\\hline\end{array}
$$

$$
\begin{array}{r}9\\+9\\\hline\end{array}\qquad
\begin{array}{r}2\\+9\\\hline\end{array}\qquad
\begin{array}{r}7\\+2\\\hline\end{array}\qquad
\begin{array}{r}3\\+7\\\hline\end{array}\qquad
\begin{array}{r}7\\+7\\\hline\end{array}
$$

$$
\begin{array}{r}5\\+4\\\hline\end{array}\qquad
\begin{array}{r}4\\+6\\\hline\end{array}\qquad
\begin{array}{r}3\\+3\\\hline\end{array}\qquad
\begin{array}{r}4\\+3\\\hline\end{array}\qquad
\begin{array}{r}8\\+2\\\hline\end{array}
$$

$$
\begin{array}{r}6\\+6\\\hline\end{array}\qquad
\begin{array}{r}7\\+8\\\hline\end{array}\qquad
\begin{array}{r}9\\+0\\\hline\end{array}\qquad
\begin{array}{r}5\\+9\\\hline\end{array}\qquad
\begin{array}{r}3\\+9\\\hline\end{array}
$$

$$
\begin{array}{r}3\\+7\\\hline\end{array}\qquad
\begin{array}{r}4\\+9\\\hline\end{array}\qquad
\begin{array}{r}0\\+5\\\hline\end{array}\qquad
\begin{array}{r}8\\+8\\\hline\end{array}\qquad
\begin{array}{r}9\\+6\\\hline\end{array}
$$

Score: _____

Name _____

Date _____

1. Selina has 6 dimes. Rhonda has 9 nickels. How much money does each girl have?

   Selina _____   Rhonda _____

   Who has more money? _____

2. Beth is putting some numbers in order from smallest to largest. Which number in the box should she put between **43** and **67**?

41	58	35	69

   $\underline{\quad 43 \quad}$ $\underline{\qquad\qquad}$ $\underline{\quad 67 \quad}$
   smallest   largest

3. Put a dot inside each angle. Count the number of angles in each shape.

   _____ angles   _____ angles   _____ angles

4. How much money is this? _____

5. Measure each line segment using inches.

   _____ "

   _____ "   _____ "

   _____ "

Name _____

Date _____

1.   Albert has 7 nickels. Luis has 3 dimes. How much money does each boy have?

   Albert _____   Luis _____

   Who has more money? _____

2.   Nora is putting some numbers in order
   from smallest to largest. Which number
   in the box should she put between **57**
   and **82**?

48	84	53	71

   ____57____   _____   ____82____
   smallest   largest

3.   Put a dot inside each angle. Count the number of angles in each shape.

   _____ angles   _____ angles   _____ angles

4.   How much money is this? _____

5.   Finish the number patterns.

   295, 296, 297, 298, ____, ____, ____, ____, ____, ____

   50, 45, 40, 35, ____, ____, ____, ____, ____, ____

   105, 106, 107, ____, ____, ____, ____, ____, ____, ____

7	5	4	8	3
+ 5	+ 3	+ 7	+ 5	+ 6

6	7	8	3	7
+ 8	+ 4	+ 3	+ 5	+ 5

6	5	8	4	8
+ 3	+ 7	+ 6	+ 7	+ 5

3	5	6	7	3
+ 8	+ 3	+ 8	+ 4	+ 6

8	6	3	8	3
+ 5	+ 3	+ 5	+ 6	+ 8

Score: _____

Name _____

Date _____

Write a number sentence for the story. Write the answer with a label.

1. Four children chose red apples, six children chose green apples, and five children chose oranges. How many children chose apples?

   Number sentence _____

   Answer _____

2. Circle the numbers that are between **25** and **37**.
   Put an X on the number that is not between **25** and **37**.

   | 27 | 31 | 34 | 39 | 26 |

3. Someone drew a line of symmetry in each shape. Circle the shape with the incorrect line of symmetry.

4. Find each answer.

   42 + 10 = _____

   36 − 10 = _____

   58
   + 10
   ——

   63
   − 10
   ——

   24
   + 10
   ——

   71
   − 10
   ——

5. Color three fourths green.
   Color three eighths yellow.
   Color one half red.

6. What time is shown on the clock?

   What time was it one hour ago?

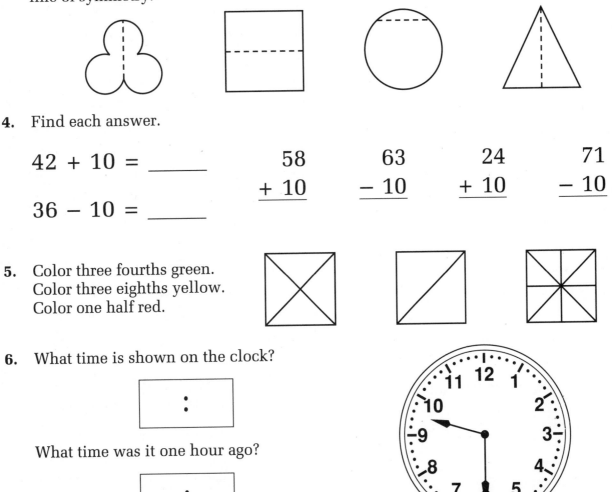

Name _____ **LESSON 58B**
                                                Math 2
Date _____

Write a number sentence for the story. Write the answer with a label.

1. Seven children chose chocolate chip cookies, three children chose ice cream, and eight children chose peanut butter cookies. How many children chose cookies?

   Number sentence _____

   Answer _____

2. Circle the numbers that are between **46** and **55**.
   Put an X on the number that is not between **46** and **55**.

   | 54   47   50   49   43 |

3. Someone drew a line of symmetry in each shape. Circle the shape with the incorrect line of symmetry.

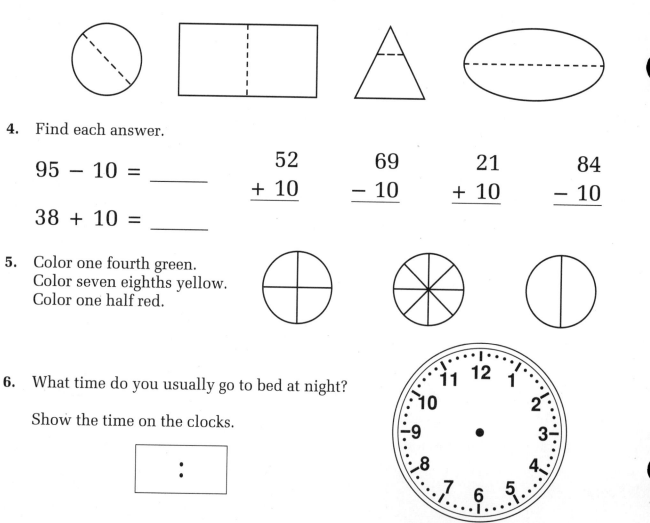

4. Find each answer.

   $95 - 10 =$ _____

   $38 + 10 =$ _____

   | 52 | 69 | 21 | 84 |
   | + 10 | − 10 | + 10 | − 10 |

5. Color one fourth green.
   Color seven eighths yellow.
   Color one half red.

6. What time do you usually go to bed at night?

   Show the time on the clocks.

7	5	4	8	3
+ 5	+ 3	+ 7	+ 5	+ 6

6	7	8	3	7
+ 8	+ 4	+ 3	+ 5	+ 5

6	5	8	4	8
+ 3	+ 7	+ 6	+ 7	+ 5

3	5	6	7	3
+ 8	+ 3	+ 8	+ 4	+ 6

8	6	3	8	3
+ 5	+ 3	+ 5	+ 6	+ 8

Score: _____

Name _____

Date _____

Write a number sentence for the story. Write the answer with a label.

1. Forty-seven children were on the bus. Ten children got off at the first stop. How many children are on the bus now?

   Number sentence _____ Answer _____

2. Number the number line using the even numbers.

   ←——+——+——+——+——+——+——+——+——+——+——→

      0   2

   Put a point at **12**. Label it **A**.
   Put a point at **8**. Label it **B**.

3. Draw a line to the correct picture.

   one fourth   •

   five eighths   •

   one third   •

   three fourths •

4. Find each answer.

   46 + 10 = _____   63 − 10 = _____

   27 + 10 = _____   48 − 10 = _____

   10 more than 31 = _____   10 less than 57 = _____

   10 more than 72 = _____   10 less than 84 = _____

5. Using tally marks, show the number of children in your class.

   [   ]

6. Write the numbers in order from smallest to largest.

   | 65   54   63 | _____ _____ _____

                    smallest   largest

Name _____

Date _____

Write a number sentence for the story. Write the answer with a label.

1. Thirty-seven children were on the bus. Ten children got off at the first stop. How many children are on the bus now?

    Number sentence _____ Answer _____

2. Number the number line using the even numbers.

    0   2

    Put a point at **14**. Label it **C**.
    Put a point at **6**. Label it **D**.

3. Draw a line to the correct picture.

    one fourth •

    two thirds •

    three eighths •

    two fourths •

4. Find each answer.

    29 + 10 = _____   92 − 10 = _____

    73 + 10 = _____   71 − 10 = _____

    10 more than 42 = _____   10 less than 38 = _____

    10 more than 55 = _____   10 less than 56 = _____

5. Using tally marks, show the number of lights in your house.

    _____

6. Write the numbers in order from smallest to largest.

    | 86   81   74 | _____ _____ _____
                            smallest   largest

Write a number sentence for the story. Write the answer with a label.

1. The children in Mrs. Rafone's class had a picnic. Each child chose a hot dog or a hamburger for lunch. Sixteen children ate a hamburger and ten children ate a hotdog. How many children were at the picnic?

    Number sentence _____

    Answer _____

2. Draw a line of symmetry in each shape or letter.

3. How much money is this? _____

    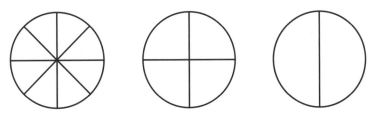

4. Color three fourths green.
    Color five eighths yellow.
    Color one half blue.

5. Find each answer.

    43 + 10 = ____   40 − 10 = ____   18   47
                                            + 10   − 10
                                            ____   ____
    29 − 10 = ____   17 + 10 = ____

6. Fill in the missing numbers. Use the fewest number of pennies possible.

    5 dimes and 13 pennies = _____ dimes + _____ pennies = _____ ¢

Name _____

Name _____

7 + 5	5 + 3	4 + 7	8 + 5	3 + 6
6 + 8	7 + 4	8 + 3	3 + 5	7 + 5
6 + 3	5 + 7	8 + 6	4 + 7	8 + 5
3 + 8	5 + 3	6 + 8	7 + 4	3 + 6
8 + 5	6 + 3	3 + 5	8 + 6	3 + 8

Score: _____

2-60Fa

5 − 0	6 − 6	10 − 5	1 − 0	7 − 1
14 − 7	5 − 1	7 − 0	4 − 2	9 − 9
9 − 1	8 − 0	18 − 9	3 − 3	2 − 0
16 − 8	3 − 1	5 − 5	6 − 0	12 − 6
6 − 1	9 − 0	6 − 3	8 − 8	4 − 1

Score: _____

1. Joe had 4 dimes. His mother gave him 4 more dimes. Write a number sentence to show how many dimes he has now.

   Number sentence _____ Answer _____

   How much money is that? _____

2. Use the graph to answer the questions.

   How many children's
   names are on this graph? _____

   How many children like bananas? _____

   How many children
   like only grapefruit? _____

   How many children like
   both bananas and grapefruit? _____

   Fruits We Like

   Bananas   Grapefruit

   Amy
   Ann   John   Mary
   Sam   Max
   Steve Sue

   What does Amy like? _____

3. Number the number line using the odd numbers.

   ←——+——+——+——+——+——+——+——+——+——+——+——→
       1

   Put a point at **9**. Label it **M**. Put a point at **15**. Label it **P**.

4. Measure each line segment using inches.

   vertical line segment _____

   horizontal line segment _____   oblique line segment _____

5. Circle the shape that is congruent to the shape on the left.

Name _____

Date _____

1. Micky had 3 dimes. His brother gave him 2 more dimes. Write a number sentence to show how many dimes he has now.

    Number sentence _____ Answer _____

    How much money is that? _____

2. Use the graph to answer the questions.

    How many children like grapefruit? _____

    How many children like only bananas? _____

    What does Mary like? _____

    What does Max like? _____

    ```
    ┌─────────────────────────────┐
    │        Fruits We Like        │
    │                              │
    │   Bananas      Grapefruit    │
    │      Amy                     │
    │                    Mary      │
    │   Ann    John                │
    │                              │
    │   Sam    Max                 │
    │                              │
    │   Steve  Sue                 │
    └─────────────────────────────┘
    ```

3. Number the number line using the odd numbers.

    Put a point at **7**. Label it **T**. Put a point at **11**. Label it **V**.

4. Finish the number patterns.

    66, 67, 68, _____, _____, _____, _____, _____, _____

    20, 18, 16, _____, _____, _____, _____, _____, _____, _____

    5, 10, 15, _____, _____, _____, _____, _____, _____, _____

5. Circle the shape that is congruent to the shape on the left.

Name _____

A 8.1

```
  7      5      4      8      3
+ 5    + 3    + 7    + 5    + 6
```

```
  6      7      8      3      7
+ 8    + 4    + 3    + 5    + 5
```

```
  6      5      8      4      8
+ 3    + 7    + 6    + 7    + 5
```

```
  3      5      6      7      3
+ 8    + 3    + 8    + 4    + 6
```

```
  8      6      3      8      3
+ 5    + 3    + 5    + 6    + 8
```

Score: _____

2-62Fa

Copyright by Saxon Publishers, Inc. and Nancy Larson. Reproduction prohibited.

Name _____

Date _____

1. Mrs. Reilly wore a different pair of earrings to school each day last week. Draw a picture to show the earrings she wore.

   How many pairs of earrings did she wear?

   _____ pairs of earrings

   How many earrings is that? _____ earrings

2. Draw a line of symmetry in each shape.

   Color the shape with 4 angles green.
   Color the shape with 5 angles yellow.
   Color the shape with 3 angles orange.

3. Use the graph to answer the questions.

   How many children's
   names are on this graph? _____

   How many children like apples? _____

   How many children like only grapes? _____

   How many children like
   both grapes and apples? _____

   What does Rose like? _____

   Fruits We Like

   Grapes   Apples

   Pete   Rose   Art
           Bob   Dave
                   Beth

4. Find each answer.

   $6 + 1 =$ _____ $9 - 1 =$ _____ $42 + 10 =$ _____ $51 - 10 =$ _____

   one more than $26 =$ _____   ten more than $28 =$ _____

   one less than $39 =$ _____   ten less than $49 =$ _____

5. Write these numbers in order from smallest to largest.

   | 49 | 47 | 43 | 46 |

   _____ _____ _____ _____
   smallest   largest

Name _____

Date _____

1. Melvin wears a different pair of socks each day. Draw a picture to show the pairs of socks he wore last week.

   (Remember, there are _____ days in one week.)

   How many pairs of socks is that? _____ pairs of socks

   How many socks is that? _____ socks

2. Draw a line of symmetry in each shape.

   Color the shape with **4** angles green.
   Color the shape with **5** angles yellow.
   Color the shape with **3** angles orange.

3. Use the graph to answer the questions.

   How many children like grapes? _____

   How many children like only apples? _____

   What does Art like? _____

   What does Beth like? _____

   Fruits We Like

   Grapes   Apples

   Pete   Rose   Art
          Bob   Dave
                 Beth

4. Find each answer.

   $8 + 1 =$ _____ $7 - 1 =$ _____ $56 + 10 =$ _____ $64 - 10 =$ _____

   one more than 52 = _____   ten more than 61 = _____

   one less than 30 = _____   ten less than 40 = _____

5. Write these numbers in order from smallest to largest.

   | 56 | 54 | 59 | 51 |

   _____ _____ _____ _____
   smallest   largest

2-62Wb

2 + 8	3 + 5	5 + 6	8 + 3	6 + 8
3 + 4	7 + 7	1 + 9	6 + 3	4 + 5
5 + 7	6 + 9	3 + 4	9 + 9	8 + 5
6 + 7	7 + 4	8 + 9	3 + 7	5 + 3
4 + 4	6 + 5	3 + 6	8 + 3	7 + 6

Score: _____

1. One of these names is my mother's name. Use the clues to find my mother's name.

   It does not have six letters.
   It does not begin with a vowel.
   It is not first.
   It is not fifth.
   Circle my mother's name.

   | Mary | Bernice | Louise | Anna | Cora |

2. Draw one dozen donuts.
   Your sister ate half a dozen donuts.
   Put an X on the ones she ate.

   How many donuts are left? _____

3. Use a red crayon to color all the shapes that are congruent to the shape on the left.

4. It is 8:30 in the morning. Is it a.m. or p.m.? _____

   Show the time on the clock.

5. About how long is a new pencil?

   7 inches   15 inches   1 inch   24 inches

6. What coins could you use to make **27¢**?

   _____

Name _____

Date _____

1. Make up your own clues for a puzzle question. Write your mother's name in one box. Write two other names in the other boxes. Write two clues.

   [ ]   [ ]   [ ]

   1. _____

   2. _____

2. Draw a dozen eggs.
   Your brother ate two eggs for breakfast.
   Put an X on the ones he ate.

   How many eggs are left? _____

3. Use a red crayon to color all the shapes that are congruent to the shape on the left.

   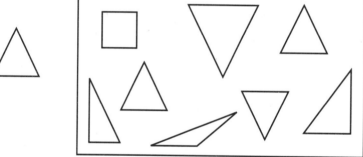

4. It is 2:30 in the afternoon. Is it a.m. or p.m.? _____

   Show the time on the clock.

   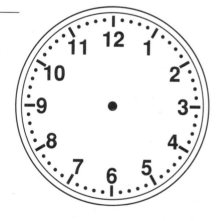

5. About how long is an egg carton?

   2 inches   6 inches   30 inches   12 inches

6. What coins could you use to make **23¢**?

   _____

$$
\begin{array}{r} 5 \\ -0 \\ \hline \end{array}
\qquad
\begin{array}{r} 6 \\ -6 \\ \hline \end{array}
\qquad
\begin{array}{r} 10 \\ -5 \\ \hline \end{array}
\qquad
\begin{array}{r} 1 \\ -0 \\ \hline \end{array}
\qquad
\begin{array}{r} 7 \\ -1 \\ \hline \end{array}
$$

$$
\begin{array}{r} 14 \\ -7 \\ \hline \end{array}
\qquad
\begin{array}{r} 5 \\ -1 \\ \hline \end{array}
\qquad
\begin{array}{r} 7 \\ -0 \\ \hline \end{array}
\qquad
\begin{array}{r} 4 \\ -2 \\ \hline \end{array}
\qquad
\begin{array}{r} 9 \\ -9 \\ \hline \end{array}
$$

$$
\begin{array}{r} 9 \\ -1 \\ \hline \end{array}
\qquad
\begin{array}{r} 8 \\ -0 \\ \hline \end{array}
\qquad
\begin{array}{r} 18 \\ -9 \\ \hline \end{array}
\qquad
\begin{array}{r} 3 \\ -3 \\ \hline \end{array}
\qquad
\begin{array}{r} 2 \\ -0 \\ \hline \end{array}
$$

$$
\begin{array}{r} 16 \\ -8 \\ \hline \end{array}
\qquad
\begin{array}{r} 3 \\ -1 \\ \hline \end{array}
\qquad
\begin{array}{r} 5 \\ -5 \\ \hline \end{array}
\qquad
\begin{array}{r} 6 \\ -0 \\ \hline \end{array}
\qquad
\begin{array}{r} 12 \\ -6 \\ \hline \end{array}
$$

$$
\begin{array}{r} 6 \\ -1 \\ \hline \end{array}
\qquad
\begin{array}{r} 9 \\ -0 \\ \hline \end{array}
\qquad
\begin{array}{r} 6 \\ -3 \\ \hline \end{array}
\qquad
\begin{array}{r} 8 \\ -8 \\ \hline \end{array}
\qquad
\begin{array}{r} 4 \\ -1 \\ \hline \end{array}
$$

Score: _____

Name _____   **LESSON 64A**

Math 2

Date _____

Write a number sentence for the story. Write the answer with a label.

1. John bought a dozen ice cream bars. He ate one ice cream bar. How many ice cream bars are left?

    Number sentence _____ Answer _____

2. Use the graph to answer the questions.

    How many children's
    names are on this graph? _____

    How many children have a dog? _____

    How many children have only cats? _____

    How many children
    have both a cat and a dog? _____

    What pet does Mike have? _____

    Children's Pets

    Dogs   Cats

    Dan   Tom   Bill
                Mike
    Ellen   Nan
                Kim

3. How much money is in each pocket? Circle the pocket with the most money.

    8 nickels   54 pennies   4 dimes
                                            7 pennies

    _____   _____   _____

4. Find the answers. Look for 10's.

    $6 + 3 + 4 + 5 + 5 =$ _____

    $$\begin{array}{r} 3 \\ 4 \\ 7 \\ + 1 \\ \hline \end{array}$$

    $2 + 8 + 1 + 7 + 9 =$ _____

5. It is morning.
    What time is it?

    _____

    It is evening.
    What time is it?

    _____

Name _____   **LESSON 64B**
                                                            Math 2
Date _____

Write a number sentence for the story. Write the answer with a label.

1. Mr. Brandon bought a dozen donuts. He ate two on the way home. How many donuts are left?

    Number sentence _____ Answer _____

2. Use the graph to answer the questions.

    How many children have a cat? _____

    How many children have only dogs? _____

    What pet does Ellen have? _____

    What pet does Nan have? _____

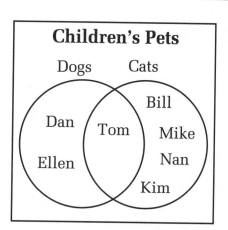

Children's Pets

Dogs   Cats

Dan Tom Bill
          Mike
Ellen   Nan
     Kim

3. How much money is in each pocket? Circle the pocket with the most money.

7 nickels

32 pennies

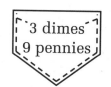
3 dimes
9 pennies

    _____   _____   _____

4. Find the answers. Look for 10's.

    7 + 3 + 2 + 9 + 1 = _____

    $$\begin{array}{r} 7 \\ 7 \\ +\ 3 \\ \hline \end{array}$$

    5 + 5 + 4 + 3 + 6 = _____

5. It is morning.
    What time is it?   It is evening.
                                        What time is it?

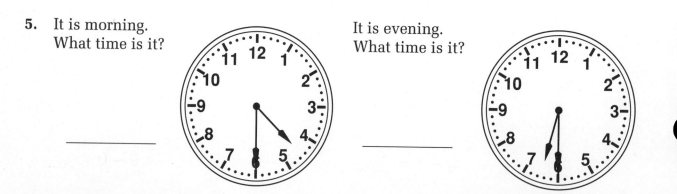

    _____   _____

Name _____

Date _____

Write a number sentence for the story. Write the answer with a label.

1. Daniel had four nickels. Roseann gave him five more nickels. How many nickels does he have now?

    Number sentence _____

    Answer _____

2. Number the number line.
    Put a point at **3**. Label it **A**.
    Put a point at **6**. Label it **B**.

    ←——+———+———+———+———+———+———+———→
         0

3. How much money is this? _____

4. Circle the largest number.
    Put an X on the smallest number.
    Write the numbers in order from smallest to largest.

47	45	52

    _____   _____   _____
    smallest   largest

5. Fill in the missing numbers on this piece of a hundred number chart.

			56		
		65			68

6. Find the answers.

    $7 - 7 =$ _____ $8 - 1 =$ _____ $12 - 6 =$ _____ $9 - 0 =$ _____

2-65Aa

2 + 8	3 + 5	5 + 6	8 + 3	6 + 8
3 + 4	7 + 7	1 + 9	6 + 3	4 + 5
5 + 7	6 + 9	3 + 4	9 + 9	8 + 5
6 + 7	7 + 4	8 + 9	3 + 7	5 + 3
4 + 4	6 + 5	3 + 6	8 + 3	7 + 6

Score: _____

2-65Fa

1. Raquel had 3 dimes and 4 pennies. Her sister gave her 2 dimes.

   How many dimes does she have now? _____

   How many pennies does she have now? _____

   How much money is this? _____

2. Label each piece using a fraction.

   Color $\frac{1}{2}$ blue.

   Color $\frac{1}{4}$ red.

   Color $\frac{1}{3}$ yellow.

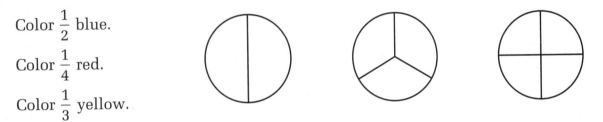

3. Cheryl has a dozen apples and a half dozen oranges. Draw the fruit.

4. Put these numbers in order from smallest to largest.

   | 23 | 47 | 50 | 32 |

   ____ ____ ____ ____
   smallest   largest

5. Show half past three in the morning.
   Write the digital time.

   _____

6. Find the answers. Look for 10's.

   $8 + 5 + 2 + 3 + 5 =$ _____ $4 + 7 + 1 + 3 + 6 =$ _____

2-65Wa

Name _____ **LESSON 65B**

Date _____ *Math 2*

1. Willie had 6 dimes and 5 pennies. His sister gave him 3 dimes.

   How many dimes does he have now? _____

   How many pennies does he have now? _____

   How much money is this? _____

2. Label each piece using a fraction.

   Color $\frac{1}{2}$ blue.

   Color $\frac{1}{4}$ red.

   Color $\frac{1}{3}$ yellow.

3. Curtis has a half dozen peaches and a dozen bananas. Draw the fruit.

4. Put these numbers in order from smallest to largest.

   | 35 | 41 | 17 | 58 |

   _____ _____ _____ _____
   smallest   largest

5. Show half past four in the afternoon.
   Write the digital time.

   _____

6. Find the answers. Look for 10's.

   $3 + 5 + 9 + 5 + 1 =$ _____ $1 + 5 + 6 + 2 + 4 + 5 =$ _____

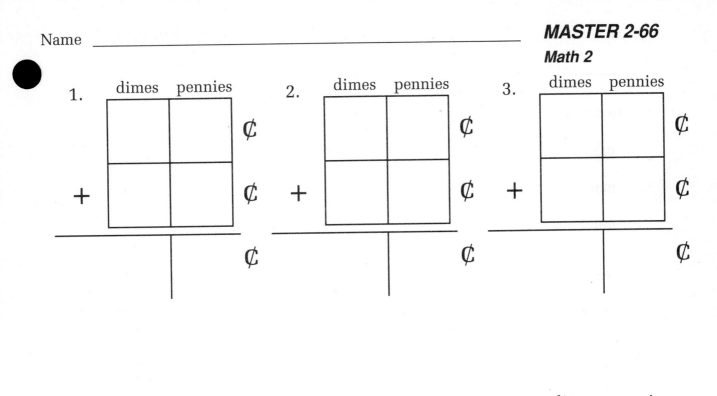

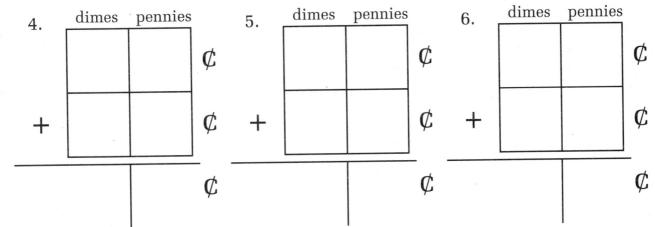

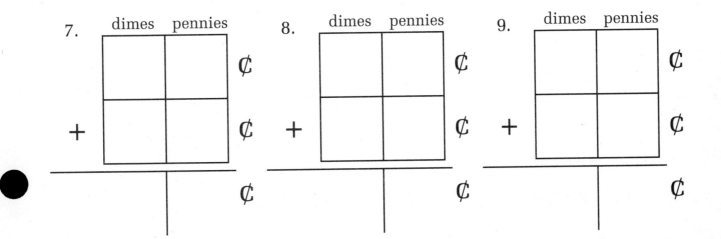

2 + 8	3 + 5	5 + 6	8 + 3	6 + 8
3 + 4	7 + 7	1 + 9	6 + 3	4 + 5
5 + 7	6 + 9	3 + 4	9 + 9	8 + 5
6 + 7	7 + 4	8 + 9	3 + 7	5 + 3
4 + 4	6 + 5	3 + 6	8 + 3	7 + 6

Score: _____

Write a number sentence for the story. Write the answer with a label.

1. On Tuesday, fifty children in Grade 2 at Washington School bought hot lunch. The other twenty-seven Grade 2 children brought their lunch from home. How many children are in Grade 2 at Washington School?

   Number sentence _____

   Answer _____

2. I have **38¢**. What coins could I have?

   _____

   What is another way to make **38¢**?

   _____

3. I have **63¢**. How many dimes and pennies is that?

   I have **24¢**. How many dimes and pennies is that?

   How many dimes and pennies is that altogether?

	dimes	pennies
+		

4. Put a dot inside each angle. Count the number of angles in each shape.

   _____ angles   _____ angles   _____ angles

5. Draw a line of symmetry in each shape in Problem 4.

6. Finish the number patterns.

   _____, _____, _____, 47, 48, 49, _____, _____, _____

   196, 197, 198, _____, _____, _____, _____, _____

Name _____   **LESSON 66B**

Date _____   *Math 2*

Write a number sentence for the story. Write the answer with a label.

1. On Tuesday, sixty-seven children in Grade 2 at Forest School bought hot lunch. The other thirty Grade 2 children brought their lunch from home. How many children are in Grade 2 at Forest School?

    Number sentence _____

    Answer _____

2. I have **32¢**. What coins could I have?

    _____

    What is another way to make **32¢**?

    _____

3. I have **34¢**. How many dimes and pennies is that?

    I have **51¢**. How many dimes and pennies is that?

    How many dimes and pennies is that altogether?

dimes	pennies

    +

4. Put a dot inside each angle. Count the number of angles in each shape.

    _____ angles   _____ angles   _____ angles

5. Draw a line of symmetry in each shape in Problem 4.

6. Finish the number patterns.

    _____, _____, _____, 63, 65, 67, _____, _____, _____

    296, 297, 298, _____, _____, _____, _____, _____